I0012117

AZ-104 Exam

400 Questions for Guaranteed Success

1st Edition

www.versatileread.com

Document Control

Proposal Name	:	AZ-104 Exam: 400 Questions for Guaranteed Success
Document Edition	:	1st
Document Release Date	:	11th September 2024
Reference	:	AZ-104
VR Product Code	:	20244402AZ104

Feedback:

If you have any comments regarding the quality of this book or otherwise alter it to better suit your needs, you can contact us through email at info@versatileread.com

Please make sure to include the book's title and ISBN in your message.

VERSAtile Reads

Voice of the Customer: Thank you for choosing this VersatileRead.com product! We highly value your feedback and insights via email to info@versatileread.com. As a token of appreciation, an amazing discount for your next purchase will be sent in response to your email.

About the Contributor:

Muniza Kamran

Muniza Kamran is a technical content developer in a professional field. She crafts clear and informative content that simplifies complex technical concepts for diverse audiences, with a passion for technology. Her expertise lies in Microsoft, cybersecurity, cloud security, and emerging technologies, making her a valuable asset in the tech industry. Her dedication to quality and accuracy ensures that her writing empowers readers with valuable insights and knowledge. She has done certification in SQL database, database design, cloud solution architecture, and NDG Linux unhatched from CISCO.

Table of Contents

About AZ-104 Certification

Introduction

The AZ-104 certification, also known as Microsoft Azure Administrator Associate, validates skills in managing and implementing Azure services. It covers a range of essential tasks such as managing identities, implementing storage solutions, deploying virtual machines, configuring virtual networks, and monitoring resources. This certification is highly valued in the industry as it demonstrates proficiency in Azure administration. It makes certified professionals sought after for roles ranging from Azure administrators and support engineers to cloud architects and security specialists. It's an ideal certification for IT professionals looking to advance their careers in cloud computing with a focus on Microsoft Azure.

What is AZ-104?

Microsoft Azure offers the Microsoft Azure Administrator Associate (AZ-104) certification and validates an individual's expertise in implementing, managing, and monitoring an organization's Microsoft Azure environment. The responsibilities of an Azure Administrator include managing Azure identities and governance, implementing and managing storage, deploying and managing Azure compute resources, configuring and managing virtual networking, and monitoring and backing up Azure resources. Key competencies involve a deep understanding of Azure infrastructure management, security and compliance, storage solutions, compute services, networking configurations, and monitoring and troubleshooting Azure environments.

Why should you take AZ-104?

Taking the AZ-104 exam and earning the Microsoft Azure Administrator Associate certification offers several compelling reasons:

- **Validation of Azure Skills**: AZ-104 certification validates your ability to manage and implement Azure services. It demonstrates to employers and peers that you possess the skills needed to administer Azure environments effectively.
- **Career Advancement:** Certification can open doors to new career opportunities or advancement within your current organization. Azure skills are in high demand, and certified professionals are sought after by employers looking to adopt or expand Azure-based solutions.
- **Industry Recognition**: Being Azure certified enhances your professional credibility and establishes you as a recognized expert in Azure administration within the industry.
- **Hands-on Experience**: Preparation for AZ-104 involves gaining practical experience with Azure services through labs and real-world scenarios. This hands-on learning is invaluable for mastering cloud administration skills.
- **Stay Current with Azure**: Azure is continually evolving with new features and services. Certification requires you to stay updated with the latest Azure technologies and best practices, keeping your skills relevant in a rapidly changing field.
- **Community and Networking**: Joining the community of Azure-certified professionals allows you to network with peers, share knowledge, and stay informed about industry trends and job opportunities.
- **Personal Growth:** Pursuing AZ-104 encourages continuous learning and personal growth. It challenges you to expand your knowledge and problem-solving abilities in cloud administration, which can be applied across various IT roles and projects.

Prerequisites for the AZ-104 exam

The Microsoft Azure Administrator Associate (AZ-104) exam doesn't have strict prerequisites in terms of required experience or previous certifications. However, candidates should have a basic understanding of cloud infrastructure principles and familiarity with Microsoft Azure services.

The Intended Audience for the AZ-104 Certification Course?

The intended audience for the Microsoft Azure Administrator Associate (AZ-104) certification course includes the following:

- **Azure Administrators**: IT professionals who manage cloud services that span storage, security, networking, and compute cloud capabilities within Microsoft Azure.
- **System Administrators**: Those looking to expand their skills to include Azure cloud administration.
- **Cloud Administrators:** Individuals responsible for managing and maintaining Azure environments.
- **IT Professionals**: Those seeking to validate their skills and knowledge in managing Azure services and infrastructure.
- **Azure Solution Architects:** Professionals who want to gain a deeper understanding of the operational aspects of Azure to better design and architect solutions.
- **DevOps Engineers:** Engineers focused on deployment, management, and operations who want to ensure their solutions are efficiently managed on Azure.
- **Technical Support Engineers**: Those providing support and troubleshooting for Azure services and looking to deepen their technical expertise.

The Certification Exam

The Microsoft Azure Administrator Associate (AZ-104) certification exam evaluates candidates' abilities to manage cloud services that span storage, security, networking, and compute cloud capabilities within Microsoft Azure. The exam covers the following key areas:

1. **Manage Azure identities and governance:**

- Manage Entra ID (Azure AD) objects, such as users, groups, and devices.
- Manage role-based access control (RBAC).
- Manage subscriptions and governance, including resource groups and Azure policies.

2. **Implement and manage storage:**

- Configure and manage Azure Blob Storage, Azure Files, and storage accounts.
- Secure storage with shared access signatures, Azure AD, and access policies.
- Implement Azure backup and restore services.

3. **Deploy and manage Azure compute resources:**

- Create and configure virtual machines (VMs) for Windows and Linux.
- Automate deployment of VMs using ARM templates.
- Configure and manage Azure App Services and container services.

4. **Configure and manage virtual networking:**

- Implement and manage virtual networks (VNets) and subnets.
- Configure network security groups (NSGs), Azure Firewall, and VPN gateways.
- Implement load balancing and monitor network performance.

5. **Monitor and back up Azure resources:**

- Monitor resources using Azure Monitor and Log Analytics.
- Implement and configure backup and recovery solutions.
- Use Azure Service Health for monitoring and managing service issues.

Exam Preparation

Before Exam

To prepare for the Microsoft Azure Administrator Associate (AZ-104) certification exam, start by reviewing the exam guide provided by Microsoft. Then, use various resources such as whitepapers, official documentation, online courses, and practice exams to reinforce your understanding of key concepts. Hands-on experience and regular self-assessment are crucial for success. Stay updated on exam changes and adjust your study plan accordingly.

Day of Exam

Preparing for the Microsoft Azure Administrator Associate (AZ-104) exam demands thorough preparation and focus. On exam day, ensure to arrive early at the testing center for smooth check-in procedures. Bring all required documents, including valid identification and any materials specified by the exam center.

During the exam, maintain a composed and focused mindset. Manage any nervousness by taking deep breaths and carefully reading each question to understand its requirements fully. Stay confident in your abilities and manage your time effectively. If faced with challenging questions, consider flagging them for later review if time permits.

After Exam

After finishing the Microsoft Azure Administrator Associate (AZ-104) exam, it's crucial to assess your performance. Identify your strengths and areas needing improvement. If allowed, review missed questions to understand why you answered them incorrectly and learn from those mistakes. This reflective process enhances your understanding and prepares you better for future exams or real-world applications.

VERSAtile Reads

Exam Information

Prior Certification		Exam Validity	
Not Required		1 Year	
Exam Fee		Exam Duration	
$165 USD		150 Minutes	
No. of Questions		Passing Marks	
40-60 Questions		700	

Recommended Experience

6+ months of hands-On experience administering Azure

Exam Format

Multiple Choice, Drag & drop, Case studies, Multiple response

AZ-104 Exam Preparation Pointers

1. **Understand the Exam Guide**: Begin your preparation by thoroughly reviewing the official AZ-104 exam guide provided by Microsoft. Understand the exam domains, objectives, and the weighting of each section.

2. **Utilize Study Resources:** Utilize a variety of resources such as Microsoft documentation, official Azure whitepapers, online courses from platforms like Pluralsight or Udemy, and practice exams. Focus on mastering core Azure services and administrative tasks.

3. **Hands-on Experience:** Gain practical experience by actively working with Azure services. Set up a free Azure account to practice tasks such as deploying virtual machines (VMs), configuring virtual networks, managing Entra ID, and implementing Azure storage solutions.

4. **Practice Exams:** Regularly test your knowledge with practice exams and quizzes. These will help familiarize you with the exam format and identify areas where you may need additional study.

5. **Time Management:** Practice effective time management both in your preparation and during the exam. Allocate time to each section based on its weighting, and learn to pace yourself to ensure you can complete all questions within the allotted time.

6. **Stay Updated:** Stay informed about any updates or changes to the AZ-104 exam blueprint. Adjust your study plan accordingly to ensure you're covering the latest Azure services, features, and best practices.

7. **Review and Reflect**: After completing practice exams or the actual AZ-104 exam, evaluate your performance. Identify strengths and areas needing improvement. Review any questions you answered incorrectly to understand the concepts better and refine your knowledge.

Job Opportunities with AZ-104 Certifications

The AZ-104 Microsoft Azure Administrator certification validates your ability to manage and administer Azure cloud services. It signifies a strong understanding of Azure infrastructure, security, and deployment models. Here's a breakdown of potential career paths with this certification:

Azure Administrator Roles:

- **Junior Azure Administrator:** Providing day-to-day administration tasks for Azure resources, including user management, resource creation/configuration, and basic troubleshooting.

- **Azure Support Engineer:** Assisting users with Azure-related issues, troubleshooting problems, and escalating complex issues to senior engineers.

- **Cloud Infrastructure Administrator (Azure Focus):** Managing and optimizing Azure infrastructure, ensuring high availability, scalability, and security.

- **Azure Cloud Administrator:** Performing a wider range of administrative tasks on Azure, including security configuration, automation, and cost management.

Cloud DevOps and Engineering Roles (Azure Focus):

- **Azure DevOps Engineer:** Creating and managing CI/CD pipelines for deploying applications to Azure, leveraging tools like Azure DevOps.
- **Cloud Solutions Architect (Azure):** Collaborating with stakeholders to design and implement cloud solutions on Azure, considering scalability, security, and cost.
- **Cloud Security Engineer (Azure):** Implementing security best practices and controls to protect Azure resources and data, ensuring compliance with regulations.

Other Potential Opportunities:

- **Cloud Migration Specialist:** Planning and executing cloud migration strategies to Azure, ensuring a smooth transition from on-premises infrastructure.
- **Cloud Cost Optimization Specialist:** Analyzing and optimizing cloud resource utilization on Azure to control costs and avoid unnecessary spending.
- **Business Analyst (Cloud Focus):** Understanding cloud concepts and Azure functionalities to analyze business needs and identify potential solutions on the platform.

Demand for AZ-104 Certification in 2024

The demand for the AZ-104 Microsoft Azure Administrator certification is expected to stay strong in 2024 for several reasons:

- **Rising Azure Adoption:** Microsoft Azure remains a dominant player in the cloud computing market, with businesses increasingly migrating workloads and deploying applications on Azure. This growth fuels the need for skilled professionals who can manage and administer this complex platform.
- **Focus on Azure Administration:** The AZ-104 specifically validates your ability to handle Azure administration tasks. This targeted skillset is highly sought-after by companies seeking to manage their Azure infrastructure effectively and securely.

- **Bridge to Advanced Roles:** The AZ-104 serves as a springboard for more advanced Azure certifications. Earning it demonstrates a foundational understanding, making you a strong candidate for pursuing specializations like Azure security, DevOps, or cloud architecture.

Practice Questions

1. What is cloud computing?
A. Using physical hardware to store data
B. Storing data and accessing computers over the internet
C. Managing data in local servers
D. Running applications on your personal computer

2. Which of the following is not a major cloud provider?
A. Amazon
B. Google
C. Azure
D. Facebook

3. What type of pricing model does cloud computing typically use?
A. Subscription-based
B. Flat-rate
C. Pay-as-you-go
D. Lifetime license

4. What is a key benefit of cloud computing in terms of cost?
A. High upfront capital expenditure
B. Elimination of capital costs for hardware and software
C. Permanent long-term contracts
D. Mandatory annual maintenance fees

5. How does cloud computing ensure reliability for businesses?
A. By using a single data center
B. By providing data backup, disaster recovery, and business continuity
C. By relying on local storage solutions
D. By using outdated hardware

6. Which of the following best describes the consumption-based model in cloud computing?
A. Paying for resources upfront

B. Paying a fixed monthly fee regardless of usage

C. Paying only for the IT resources you use

D. Paying for a lifetime subscription

7. What is the role of auto-scaling in cloud performance predictability?

A. Reduces the number of resources during high-demand

B. Disables additional resources during low demand

C. Dynamically deploys additional resources to meet increased demand

D. Manually adjusts resource allocation

8. Which expenditure category does cloud computing fall under?

A. Capital Expenditure (CapEx)

B. Operational Expenditure (OpEx)

C. Fixed Expenditure

D. Variable Expenditure

9. How does cloud computing enhance security for organizations?

A. By using outdated security measures

B. By decentralizing data storage

C. By providing advanced security features and protecting data, applications, and infrastructure

D. By reducing the number of security protocols

10. What is a Virtual Machine (VM) in the context of cloud computing?

A. A physical computer used to run programs

B. An application running on your desktop

C. A compute resource using software to run programs and deploy apps

D. A storage device

11. Which of the following is the main advantage of SaaS (Software as a Service)?

A. Allows you to build and deploy applications

B. Provides a complete deployment environment in the cloud

C. Enables easy access to cloud-based apps without installing hardware and software

D. Offers infrastructure management and scaling

12. Which cloud service model is best suited for businesses looking to deploy computing infrastructure quickly and avoid hardware complexities?
A. SaaS
B. PaaS
C. IaaS
D. On-Premises

13. In the shared responsibility model for SaaS, who is primarily responsible for the data and information stored in the cloud?
A. The cloud provider
B. The customer
C. Both the cloud provider and the customer
D. Neither the cloud provider nor the customer

14. Which deployment model allows organizations to use a combination of on-premises and cloud resources?
A. Public Cloud
B. Private Cloud
C. Hybrid Cloud
D. Community Cloud

15. What is a key advantage of using PaaS for application development?
A. Eliminates the need for a development framework
B. Reduces deployment time with pre-coded applications
C. Provides physical hardware for computing
D. Ensures 100% data security

16. Which cloud service model offers the least amount of user responsibility for infrastructure management?
A. IaaS
B. PaaS
C. SaaS
D. On-Premises

17. Which of the following is a common scenario for using IaaS?
A. Email hosting
B. Running high-performance computing workloads
C. Providing a development framework
D. Managing the application lifecycle

18. What is a significant benefit of using PaaS for geographically distributed development teams?
A. Provides physical hardware for each team
B. Ensures all teams use the same development framework over the internet
C. Eliminates the need for internet connectivity
D. Guarantees zero latency in communication

19. In the context of cloud computing, what does "pay-as-you-go" mean?
A. You pay a fixed amount for unlimited usage
B. You pay only for the services and resources you use
C. You pay in advance for future services
D. You pay based on subscription plans

20. Which cloud deployment model is primarily managed by the cloud provider and offers lower costs, scalability, and flexibility?
A. Public Cloud
B. Private Cloud
C. Hybrid Cloud
D. Community Cloud

21. What is a data center in the context of Azure?
A. A facility that provides customer support
B. A physical facility that hosts network servers and infrastructure for Azure services
C. A regional office for sales and marketing
D. A cloud-based storage solution

22. What is a key benefit of Azure's global regions?
A. They reduce the cost of services

B. They ensure data residency and compliance

C. They limit the geographic reach of services

D. They increase customer support options

23. How many regions does Azure have available around the world?

A. 100

B. 54

C. 72

D. 140

24. When choosing an Azure region, which of the following is not a primary consideration?

A. Location

B. Features

C. Price

D. Customer support availability

25. What is an Azure "Availability Zone"?

A. A set of regions within a geography

B. A location within a region that is physically separate and independently powered

C. A backup service for disaster recovery

D. A service to upgrade VMs automatically

26. What is the purpose of an Azure Region Pair?

A. To offer discounted pricing

B. To ensure at least one region in the pair is prioritized during outages

C. To provide customer support in multiple languages

D. To automatically upgrade services

27. What does "data residency" refer to in Azure?

A. The cost of storing data

B. The geographic location where data is physically stored

C. The performance of data retrieval

D. The backup frequency of data

28. What is an "Availability Set" in Azure?
A. A grouping of VMs to be managed together
B. A set of data centers forming a region
C. A plan for automatic VM upgrades
D. A logical grouping to separate VM resources across multiple physical servers

29. Which of the following is an example of a special Azure region?
A. West US
B. East Asia
C. US Gov. Virginia
D. Central India

30. What does "Failover" mean in the context of Azure services?
A. The process of upgrading VMs
B. The ability to switch automatically to a backup system
C. The practice of reducing service costs
D. The manual backup of data

31. What is the most common way to interact with Azure?
A. Azure CLI
B. Azure PowerShell
C. Azure Portal
D. Azure Cloud Shell

32. Which tool is described as a 'text entry tool' for interacting with Azure services?
A. Azure CLI
B. Azure PowerShell
C. Azure Portal
D. Azure Cloud Shell

33. What is one of the benefits of using Azure CLI?
A. Personalizing your dashboard
B. Stable commands that rarely change

C. Quick feature updates

D. Integrated file editor

34. Which Azure tool allows you to use cmdlets to perform tasks?

A. Azure CLI

B. Azure PowerShell

C. Azure Portal

D. Azure Cloud Shell

35. How can you check the version of Azure CLI installed on your system?

A. az version

B. az --check

C. az --version

D. az check-version

36. Which Azure tool offers an integrated file editor and dedicated storage to persist data between sessions?

A. Azure CLI

B. Azure PowerShell

C. Azure Portal

D. Azure Cloud Shell

37. What command is used to create a new virtual machine in Azure PowerShell?

A. az vm create

B. New-AzVm

C. create-vm

D. New-VM

38. For which platforms is Azure CLI cross-compatible?

A. Windows only

B. Windows and Mac

C. Windows, Mac, and Linux

D. Windows, Mac, Linux, and Android

39. Which Azure tool provides access to all resources and features through a single login?
A. Azure CLI
B. Azure PowerShell
C. Azure Portal
D. Azure Cloud Shell

40. What is one of the benefits of using the Azure Portal for cost management?
A. Automated scripting
B. Secure access from anywhere
C. Monitoring current and projected costs
D. Integrated file editor

41. Which Azure service allows you to create and host web apps, mobile back-ends, and RESTful APIs without network maintenance in the programming language of your choice?
A. Azure IoT Hub
B. App Service
C. Azure Backup
D. Azure Maps

42. What purpose does the API Gateway in Azure API Management serve?
A. Acts as a bi-directional communication hub
B. Accepts API calls and routes them to the backend
C. Monitors the infrastructure and software
D. Provides backup against data loss

43. Which Azure service is specifically designed for business continuity and disaster recovery with failover and failback capabilities?
A. Azure Backup
B. Azure App Service
C. Azure Site Recovery
D. Azure Search

44. What does Microsoft Entra ID B2C provide?
A. A message hub for bi-directional communication between IoT devices
B. Consumer identity and access management for consumer-based applications
C. A cloud-based identity and access management service for internal resources
D. A feature for live application monitoring

45. Which service in Azure is used for key management in an encrypted form and provides real-time usage logs of keys?
A. Azure Monitor
B. Key Vault
C. Azure Backup
D. Microsoft Entra ID

46. Which Azure service collects and visualizes data from various sources like on-premises and cloud for interactive analysis of log queries?
A. Azure IoT Hub
B. App Service
C. Log Analytics
D. Azure Maps

47. What is the primary function of Azure Monitor?
A. Provides basic monitoring of Azure resources
B. Creates reliable and functional back-end API gateways
C. Manages policies across resources and monitors compliance
D. Sends mobile push notifications from any backend service

48. Which service in Azure IoT is a cloud-hosted managed service that functions as the main message hub for bi-directional communication between IoT solutions and devices?
A. IoT Central
B. IoT Hub
C. Device Provisioning Service (DPS)
D. Azure Sphere

49. What does Azure Cognitive Search, the only cloud search service with built-in AI capabilities, perform?
A. Full-text search using simple or lucent query syntax
B. Provides backup against data loss in the cloud
C. Connects, monitors, and controls tons of IoT assets
D. Enhances protection and security of cloud-based environments through continuous monitoring

50. What role does Microsoft Defender for Cloud play in Azure?
A. Provides location-based solutions in IoT and AI domains
B. Collects and visualizes data for interactive analysis of log queries
C. Improves the security position of data centers and provides advanced threat safety
D. Sends mobile push notifications to any platform

51. Which Azure storage type is best suited for storing large volumes of unstructured data, such as text or binary data?
A. Azure Table Storage
B. Azure Blob Storage
C. Azure Queue Storage
D. Azure Disk Storage

52. What is the maximum file share size in Azure File Storage?
A. 1TB
B. 2TB
C. 5TB
D. 10TB

53. Which Azure storage replication type provides the highest level of durability by replicating data across regions?
A. Locally Redundant Storage (LRS)
B. Zone Redundant Storage (ZRS)
C. Geo-Redundant Storage (GRS)
D. Read Access Geo-Redundant Storage (RA-GRS)

54. What is the primary use case for Azure Queue Storage?
A. Storing structured data
B. Storing asynchronous lists of messages
C. Storing large binary files
D. Storing relational databases

55. Which Azure storage service uses a schema-less design to provide a key/attribute database?
A. Azure Blob Storage
B. Azure Table Storage
C. Azure File Storage
D. Azure Disk Storage

56. What is the function of Azure Data Lake Store?
A. It is used for storing relational data
B. It is used as a repository for analytics workloads
C. It is used for caching frequently accessed data
D. It is used for message queuing

57. What is the maximum message size that can be stored in Azure Queue Storage?
A. 8 KB
B. 32 KB
C. 64 KB
D. 128 KB

58. Which of the following services is part of Azure's Big Data and Analytics tools and is an open-source managed analytic service?
A. Azure Data Factory
B. Azure SQL Data Warehouse
C. Azure HDInsight
D. Azure Analysis Service

59. Which Azure database service provides turnkey global replication and supports multiple models like SQL, MongoDB, and Cassandra?
A. Azure SQL DB

B. Azure Cosmos DB

C. Azure Database for PostgreSQL

D. Azure Redis Cache

60. What is the purpose of Azure Redis Cache?

A. To store large amounts of unstructured data

B. To provide a managed in-memory cache service

C. To store and manage relational databases

D. To provide a schema-less database design

61. What is a resource in Azure?

A. A container for organizing other containers

B. A manageable item available in Azure, such as a VM, storage, or database

C. A set of guidelines for managing Azure services

D. A JSON file that defines dependencies between resources

62. What is the primary function of a Resource Group in Azure?

A. To provide a billing summary

B. To authenticate and authorize access to Azure services

C. To deploy and manage resources in a container-like structure

D. To create REST operations for Azure services

63. What happens when you delete a Resource Group?

A. The resources within it remain unaffected

B. It only deletes the Resource Group metadata

C. All resources within the Resource Group are also deleted

D. It converts the Resource Group into a read-only state

64. Which of the following is not a feature of Azure Resource Manager?

A. Access Control

B. Tagging for easier identification

C. Billing Boundary enforcement

D. Consistent deployment of resources

65. What is the role of Azure Resource Provider?
A. To define the lifecycle of a resource
B. To supply resources for the Resource Manager
C. To control billing and access management
D. To create Resource Groups

66. What file format is used for Resource Manager Templates?
A. XML
B. YAML
C. JSON
D. CSV

67. Which feature allows you to prevent resources from being deleted accidentally?
A. Role-Based Access Control (RBAC)
B. Resource Locks
C. Resource Tags
D. Billing Subscriptions

68. What is the purpose of using Tags in Azure?
A. To enforce access control policies
B. To organize resources by usage, type, or location
C. To associate custom details with a resource or resource group
D. To create REST operations for Azure services

69. What is an Azure Subscription primarily used for?
A. To group similar resources by usage
B. To create Resource Groups
C. To authenticate and authorize access to Azure services
D. To define REST operations for specific Azure services

70. What requires you to create multiple Azure subscriptions?
A. Organizing resources by lifecycle
B. Enforcing consistent deployment of resources
C. Separating billing for production and development environments
D. Defining REST operations for different services

71. What does High Availability (HA) in cloud computing primarily ensure?
A. Zero downtime
B. Dynamic resource extension
C. Immediate replacement of failed servers
D. Capacity planning

72. Which cloud computing concept guarantees zero downtime by mitigating faults immediately?
A. High Availability
B. Fault Tolerance
C. Scalability
D. Elasticity

73. What is the primary focus of Disaster Recovery (DR) in cloud computing?
A. Increasing server capacity
B. Maintaining zero downtime
C. Recovering business operations after catastrophic events
D. Automatically balancing loads

74. Which term describes the ability to add or remove resources based on demand in cloud computing?
A. Elasticity
B. Scalability
C. Agility
D. Fault Tolerance

75. What is vertical scaling, also known as?
A. Scaling out
B. Scaling up
C. Horizontal scaling
D. Load balancing

76. Which cloud service model involves hosting and maintaining applications and underlying infrastructure while managing updates?

A. IaaS
B. PaaS
C. SaaS
D. Serverless

77. Which manageability approach involves deploying resources at the appropriate scale automatically as needed?
A. Management in the Cloud
B. Management of the Cloud
C. Load Balancing
D. Vertical Scaling

78. In which scaling method are additional servers added to distribute the workload across multiple servers?
A. Vertical scaling
B. Horizontal scaling
C. Elastic scaling
D. Fault Tolerance

79. Which cloud service model is designed to support the complete application life cycle, from building to updating?
A. IaaS
B. PaaS
C. SaaS
D. Serverless

80. What is the primary function of cloud governance?
A. Managing virtual machines
B. Ensuring efficient and desired cloud operations
C. Providing on-demand environments
D. Extending network resources dynamically

81. What is the primary purpose of Azure Management Groups?
A. To provide additional storage for Azure services
B. To organize subscriptions for governance and compliance

C. To manage network traffic

D. To host Virtual Machines

82. Which of the following is not a supported trigger type for Azure Logic Apps?

A. HTTP request

B. Time-based

C. Storage account

D. Azure Blob versioning

83. What feature does Azure App Service provide?

A. A fully managed platform for creating cloud applications

B. A container orchestration service

C. A private network for virtual machines

D. A load-balancing service

84. How many management groups can be supported in a single Azure directory?

A. 1,000

B. 5,000

C. 10,000

D. 50,000

85. What is Azure Batch primarily used for?

A. Running containerized applications

B. Creating and managing virtual machines

C. Batch processing jobs and running large-scale parallel and HPC applications

D. Hosting DNS domains

86 Which Azure service is best suited for managing high-bandwidth content delivery?

A. Azure DNS

B. Azure ExpressRoute

C. Azure Content Delivery Network (CDN)

D. Azure VPN Gateway

87. What is the maximum depth of a management group tree in Azure?
A. 4 layers
B. 5 layers
C. 6 layers
D. 8 layers

88. What does Azure Function's billing depend on?
A. The number of virtual machines used
B. The amount of data stored
C. The number of executions
D. The number of management groups

89. Which service provides secure, high-performance connections between Azure virtual networks and on-site locations?
A. Azure Load Balancer
B. Azure ExpressRoute
C. Azure Traffic Manager
D. Azure VPN Gateway

90. Which Azure service is used for centralized access management across multiple subscriptions?
A. Azure DNS
B. Azure Management Groups
C. Azure Batch
D. Azure CDN

91. What is an Azure region?
A. A single datacenter where Azure services are hosted
B. A specific service within Azure
C. A geographical area with multiple networked datacenters
D. The physical location of Microsoft headquarters

92. What is the main benefit of Azure having more global regions than any other cloud provider?
A. Reduced costs for Microsoft

B. Increased competition among cloud providers

C. Flexibility in bringing applications closer to users

D. Simplified management of services

93. What is an Azure geography?

A. A single Azure region

B. A global network of Azure data centers

C. A discrete market defined by geopolitical boundaries

D. A collection of Azure services

94. Why are Azure geographies important?

A. They provide unlimited storage for data

B. They ensure data residency and compliance are maintained within geographical boundaries

C. They are used to categorize different Azure services

D. They reduce the cost of Azure services globally

95. What does data residency refer to in the context of Azure?

A. The number of data centers in a region

B. The location of Microsoft's corporate offices

C. The physical or geographic location of an organization's data

D. The residency status of Azure employees

96. How does Azure ensure fault tolerance at the geographical level?

A. By limiting the number of datacenters in each region

B. Through high-capacity networking infrastructure connecting geographies

C. By offering free services

D. By using a single, centralized datacenter for backup

97. Which areas are Azure geographies broken up into?

A. North America, South America, and Central America

B. Americas, Europe, and Asia

C. Americas, Europe, Asia Pacific, Middle East, and Africa

D. Northern Hemisphere and Southern Hemisphere

98. What is the purpose of organizing Azure data centers into regions?
A. To limit the number of services Azure can offer
B. To reduce the overall cost of Azure services
C. To ensure workloads are balanced and provide scalability and redundancy
D. To restrict the use of Azure services to certain countries

99. Which of the following is a true statement about Azure regions?
A. Each Azure region is isolated from others and operates independently.
B. Azure regions do not provide redundancy for deployed services.
C. Users can directly access and choose specific datacenters within a region.
D. A region can contain multiple data centers networked together

100. What is the role of availability zones in Azure?
A. They are individual datacenters with no special significance.
B. They are unique services offered only in certain regions.
C. They are single regions that contain multiple geographies.
D. They are not mentioned in the provided context.

101. What is the main advantage of using Azure Resource Manager for managing your application infrastructure?
A. It requires manual steps for setup
B. It allows managing resources individually
C. It enables deployment, management, and monitoring of resources as a group
D. It only supports Azure CLI

102. Which of the following is not a benefit of using Azure Resource Manager?
A. Consistent deployment state across different environments
B. Imperative command requirement for resource setup
C. Role-Based Access Control (RBAC) integration
D. Ability to apply tags to resources

103. What type of syntax do Azure Resource Manager templates use?
A. Procedural syntax
B. Declarative syntax
C. Object-Oriented syntax
D. Functional syntax

104. In Azure Resource Manager, what is a "resource"?
A. A JSON file that defines infrastructure
B. An item available through Azure, such as a virtual machine or storage account
C. A container holding related resources
D. A service that supplies resources

105. What is a "resource group" in Azure?
A. A JSON file
B. A service that supplies resources
C. A container that holds related resources for an Azure solution
D. A virtual network

106. Which of the following Azure tools can interact with the Azure Resource Manager API?
A. Azure PowerShell
B. Azure CLI
C. Azure portal
D. All of the above

107. What is the role of a "resource provider" in Azure Resource Manager?
A. It holds related resources for a solution
B. It supplies operations for working with deployed resources
C. It defines the dependencies between resources
D. It applies access control

108. Which of the following is the correct format for a resource type name in Azure Resource Manager?
A. resource-provider/resource-group
B. resource-group/resource-type

C. resource-provider/resource-type

D. resource-type/resource-provider

109. What feature of Azure Resource Manager helps in clarifying an organization's billing?

A. Role-Based Access Control (RBAC)

B. Consistent management layer

C. Tags

D. Declarative templates

110. Which of the following statements is true regarding Azure Resource Manager templates?

A. They require manual steps for setup

B. They use imperative commands for deployment

C. They define infrastructure using JSON

D. They cannot be reused for different environments

111. What happens to existing resources in a resource group when you deploy additional resources?

A. They are removed and replaced by new resources

B. They remain unaffected

C. They are duplicated

D. They are moved to a new resource group

112. Which of the following statements is true about resource groups?

A. Resources can exist in multiple resource groups simultaneously

B. Resource groups can be renamed

C. Resource groups can have resources from many different regions

D. Resources cannot be moved between resource groups

113. When should you consider placing a resource in a different resource group?

A. When it needs to be deployed in the same region

B. When it shares the same lifecycle as other resources

C. When it needs to exist on a different deployment cycle

D. When it does not require any metadata

114. Why do you need to specify a location for a resource group?
A. To determine the cost of the resources
B. To ensure resources are deployed in the same region
C. To specify where the metadata is stored
D. To limit the resources to a single region

115. What is a possible consequence of not applying Resource Manager locks?
A. Resources will be automatically deleted after a month
B. An administrator may accidentally delete resources
C. Resources will not be able to interact with each other
D. Resources will be moved to a different resource group automatically

116. Which type of lock should be used if you want to prevent any changes to a resource?
A. Delete lock
B. Read-Only lock
C. Write lock
D. Full lock

117. What happens to write and delete operations on resource groups when moving resources?
A. They are allowed only on the source group
B. They are allowed only in the target group
C. They are blocked on both the source and target groups
D. They are allowed on both the source and target groups

118. Can a resource in one resource group interact with a resource in another resource group?
A. No, resources in different groups cannot interact
B. Yes, but only if they are in the same region
C. Yes, resources can interact if they are related but don't share the same lifecycle
D. No, they must be in the same resource group to interact

119. Which of the following is not a rule for resource groups?
A. Resources can only exist in one resource group
B. Resource groups can be renamed
C. Resource groups can have resources of many different types
D. Resource groups can have resources from many different regions

120. What type of lock prevents the deletion of a resource?
A. Read-Only lock
B. Write lock
C. Delete lock
D. Full lock

121. What is Azure Cloud Shell?
A. A virtual machine hosting service
B. A command-line environment accessible through a web browser
C. A cloud-based database service
D. An email hosting service

122. What advantage does Azure Cloud Shell provide regarding software updates?
A. You must manually update the software
B. It automatically updates to the latest versions
C. It never updates
D. You need to contact Microsoft support for updates

123. How can you persist files between sessions in Azure Cloud Shell?
A. Local hard drive
B. USB drive
C. Azure File Share
D. External cloud storage

124. Which of the following actions can you perform using Azure Cloud Shell?
A. Manage Azure resources
B. Watch movies

C. Send emails

D. Play games

125. What is the default encryption standard for Azure Cloud Shell's infrastructure?
A. Single encryption
B. Triple encryption
C. Double encryption at rest
D. No encryption

126. How long do Azure Cloud Shell sessions last before terminating due to inactivity?
A. 10 minutes
B. 20 minutes
C. 30 minutes
D. 60 minutes

127. Which command-line experiences can you select in Azure Cloud Shell?
A. PowerShell only
B. Bash only
C. Both PowerShell and Bash
D. CMD only

128. Can you access Azure Cloud Shell from code snippets in Microsoft Learn?
A. Yes
B. No
C. Only during business hours
D. Only with a subscription

129. If you need to access Azure Cloud Shell, which of the following is not a way to access it?
A. From a direct link
B. From the Azure portal
C. From a physical Azure store
D. From code snippets in Microsoft Learn

130. What should you do if your Azure Cloud Shell session terminates?
A. Contact Microsoft support
B. Restart your computer
C. Start a new Cloud Shell session
D. Reinstall the Azure CLI

131. Which of the following tools is not preconfigured in Azure Cloud Shell?
A. Ansible
B. Terraform
C. Chef
D. Apache Tomcat

132. What is one major limitation of Azure Cloud Shell?
A. It requires a high-speed internet connection.
B. It does not support Bash as a shell option.
C. It disconnects sessions after 20 minutes of inactivity.
D. It cannot interact with Azure resources.

133. Which command-line tools for interacting with Azure resources are available in Azure Cloud Shell?
A. Azure CLI and Azure classic CLI
B. AWS CLI and Google Cloud CLI
C. IBM Cloud CLI and Oracle Cloud CLI
D. None of the above

134. For which of the following scenarios is Azure Cloud Shell not recommended?
A. Editing scripts via the Cloud Shell editor
B. Opening multiple sessions at the same time
C. Using either Bash or PowerShell to manage Azure resources
D. Interacting with Azure resources from a browser-based device

135. Which text editors are available in Azure Cloud Shell?
A. Notepad and WordPad
B. Sublime Text and Atom

C. Vim, Nano, and Emacs

D. Visual Studio and Eclipse

136. What type of storage limitation does Azure Cloud Shell have?

A. It can only store files temporarily.

B. Storage is only available in a single region.

C. It requires external storage devices.

D. It cannot store files at all.

137. Which utility tools are available in Azure Cloud Shell?

A. Only Docker

B. Docker, Kubectl, and Helm

C. Docker, Jupyter, and Hadoop

D. None of the above

138. What happens if you need admin permissions like sudo access in Azure Cloud Shell?

A. You can request temporary sudo access.

B. Azure Cloud Shell provides full admin permissions by default.

C. You cannot obtain admin permissions in Azure Cloud Shell.

D. Only PowerShell provides sudo access.

139. Which container orchestration tools are preconfigured in Azure Cloud Shell?

A. Docker Compose and Swarm

B. Kubernetes and Mesos

C. DC/OS CLI and Kubernetes (Kubectl)

D. Docker Swarm and Nomad

140. What is a suitable use case for Azure Cloud Shell?

A. Running a web server for a production application

B. Persisting files between sessions for later use

C. Running resource-intensive simulations

D. Hosting a database with high availability

141. Which command is used to list the contents of the current working directory in Bash?
A. dir
B. ls
C. list
D. show

142. What does the `-a` flag do when used with the `ls` command?
A. Lists files in alphabetical order
B. Lists only files
C. Lists all files, including hidden ones
D. Lists all files in reverse order

143. How can you combine multiple flags in a single `ls` command?
A. ls -a -l
B. ls a l
C. ls -al
D. ls -a --l

144. What command would you use to display the manual for the `mkdir` command?
A. help mkdir
B. man mkdir
C. info mkdir
D. guide mkdir

145. What does the `mkdir --help` command do?
A. Creates a directory named `help`
B. Displays help information for the `mkdir` command
C. Opens the manual page for `mkdir`
D. Lists all directories

146. Which of the following is not a shell commonly used in Linux?
A. Bash
B. PowerShell

C. csh

D. zsh

147. What is the full form of Bash?

A. Built Again Shell

B. Bourne Again Shell

C. Basic Shell

D. Bash Automated Shell

148. According to the Unix design philosophy, which of the following is a key idea?

A. Programs should be complex and multi-functional

B. Programs should work independently

C. Programs use text streams as the universal interface

D. Programs should have graphical interfaces

149. How do you list the contents of the `/etc` directory using the `ls` command?

A. ls /etc/

B. list /etc

C. show /etc

D. dir /etc

150. What does the `man` command do in Bash?

A. Changes file permissions

B. Displays manual pages for commands

C. Creates directories

D. Lists all users

151. What does the wildcard '*' represent in Bash?

A. A single character

B. Zero or more characters

C. A digit

D. An uppercase letter

152. Which command lists all files in the current directory that end with '.png'?
A. ls *.jpg
B. ls *.jpeg
C. ls *.png
D. ls *jp*g

153. How would you list all JPEG files that have extensions '.jpg' or '.jpeg' using a single command?
A. ls *.jp*g
B. ls *.png
C. ls *jp*g
D. ls *.jpg *.jpeg

154. What does the '?' wildcard represent in Bash?
A. Zero or more characters
B. A single character
C. A lowercase letter
D. A period

155. Which command lists all files whose names start with a number?
A. ls [a-z]*
B. ls *[0-9]*
C. ls [0-9]*
D. ls [A-Z]*

156. How would you list all files that contain a period followed by either a lowercase 'j' or 'p'?
A. ls *.[jp]*
B. ls *.[JP]*
C. ls *.[j-p]*
D. ls ^.[a-z]*

157. Which command lists all files whose names begin with an uppercase letter?
A. ls [A-Z]*

B. ls [a-z]*
C. ls [0-9]*
D. ls [A-Z0-9]*

158. How can you list all files that end with a digit?
A. ls [0-9]*
B. ls *[0-9]
C. ls *[0-9]*
D. ls [a-z]*[0-9]

159. Which command lists all files in the current directory whose names contain periods followed by an uppercase or lowercase 'J' or 'P'?
A. ls *.[jp]*
B. ls *.[JP]*
C. ls *.[jpJP]*
D. ls *.[a-zA-Z]*

160. How would you escape a wildcard character like '*' in a file name search?
A. ls *.*
B. ls ***
C. ls [*]*
D. ls **

161. Which of the following is not a feature of Azure Kubernetes Service (AKS)?
A. Managed Kubernetes
B. Integrated CI/CD
C. Automated upgrades and patching
D. Built-in SQL database support

162. How do you include hidden files in the output of the `ls` command?
A. ls -h
B. ls -l
C. ls -a
D. ls -R

163. What is the purpose of the `-l` flag when used with the `ls` command?
A. To list files in long format
B. To list files in lowercase
C. To list files in reverse order
D. To list only directories

164. What does the `cat` command do?
A. Changes the current directory
B. Lists directory contents
C. Displays the contents of a file
D. Deletes a file

165. Which of the following commands will show the contents of the `os-release` file?
A. ls /etc/os-release
B. cat /etc/os-release
C. cd /etc/os-release
D. rm /etc/os-release

166. What information is not typically included in the long format output of `ls -l`?
A. File permissions
B. File owner
C. Size of the file
D. File contents

167. Which of the following directories contains system-configuration files in Linux?
A. /home
B. /tmp
C. /etc
D. /var

168. What is the significance of files and directories whose names begin with a period (.) in Linux?

A. They are system files
B. They are hidden files
C. They are read-only files
D. They are executable files

169. Which command would you use to list files and directories with detailed information, including hidden files?
A. ls -lh
B. ls -al
C. ls -l
D. ls -a

170. Which of the following is not a type of Azure Storage account?
A. General-purpose v2
B. Blob Storage
C. Queue Storage
D. SQL Storage

171. Which operator is used to redirect the output to a file but appends to the file instead of overwriting it?
A. <
B. >
C. >>
D. |

172. What command would you use to sort the contents of a file named `data.txt` and save the results in a file named `sorted_data.txt`?
A. sort data.txt > sorted_data.txt
B. sort < data.txt
C. sort < data.txt > sorted_data.txt
D. sort data.txt >> sorted_data.txt

173. Which operator is used to redirect input from a file instead of the keyboard?
A. <
B. >

C. >>

D. |

174. What does the following command do? `ps -ef | grep daemon.`
A. Lists all daemons currently running
B. Lists all processes and filters for lines containing "daemon."
C. Greps for the word 'daemon' in the current directory
D. Displays the contents of a file named 'daemon'

175. How can you list all files in the current directory and save the output in a file named `listing.txt` without overwriting the file if it already exists?
A. ls > listing.txt
B. ls < listing.txt
C. ls | listing.txt
D. ls >> listing.txt

176. If you want to see the first 10 lines of processes running, which command would you use?
A. ps -ef | more
B. ps -ef | head
C. ps -ef | grep head
D. ps -ef | tail

177. What is the purpose of the `|` operator in Bash commands?
A. To redirect input to a source other than the keyboard
B. To redirect output to a destination other than the screen
C. To append output to a file
D. To pipe output from one command to the input of another

178. Consider the command: `cat file.txt | fmt | pr | lpr`. What does `lpr` do here?
A. Formats the text into a tidy paragraph
B. Paginates the results
C. Sends the paginated output to the printer
D. Displays the contents of file.txt

179. To see output one screen at a time, which command would you use?
A. ps -ef | more
B. ps -ef > file.txt
C. ps -ef | grep daemon
D. ps -ef | head

180. What is the correct syntax to redirect both input and output in a single command?
A. cmd < input > output
B. cmd > input < output
C. cmd | input | output
D. cmd << input >> output

181. What are the two main parts of PowerShell?
A. A command-line shell and a scripting language
B. A graphical interface and a command-line shell
C. A database manager and a scripting language
D. A text editor and a command-line shell

182. Which of the following is a benefit of using a console?
A. It provides a graphical interface for easier interaction
B. It allows running batches of commands for task automation
C. It stores commands and scripts in binary files
D. It requires more manual intervention than a graphical interface

183. What is a significant advantage of storing PowerShell commands and scripts in a text file?
A. They cannot be edited once saved
B. They are not compatible with source-control systems
C. They are repeatable and auditable
D. They do not support cloud resource interaction

184. What unique feature does PowerShell offer compared to traditional command-line shells?
A. It operates only on text
B. It requires separate executables for each command

C. It operates on objects over text

D. It does not support pipelines

185. What are cmdlets in PowerShell?
A. Separate executable files for each command
B. Text-based scripts for automating tasks
C. Built-in commands based on a common runtime
D. Graphical interface tools

186. Which PowerShell feature allows users to run commands using alternate names?
A. Objects
B. Aliases
C. Pipelines
D. Scripts

187. How does PowerShell handle the output of one command as input for the next command?
A. By using graphical elements
B. By ignoring the output
C. By using a pipeline
D. By converting outputs into text

188. What are the core cmdlets in PowerShell built on?
A. Java
B. .NET Core
C. Python
D. Ruby

189. What type of commands can you extend PowerShell with?
A. Only built-in executables
B. Only graphical tools
C. Cmdlets, scripts, and functions
D. Only native executables

190. Which command type in PowerShell can be either native executables, cmdlets, functions, scripts, or aliases?
A. Database commands
B. Graphical commands
C. Shell commands
D. PowerShell commands

191. What is a cmdlet in PowerShell?
A. A compiled command that can be developed in .NET or .NET Core and invoked within PowerShell.
B. A text file used for scripting in PowerShell.
C. A type of PowerShell variable.
D. A graphical user interface for PowerShell.

192. Which cmdlet would you use to get a list of all available commands in PowerShell?
A. Get-Help
B. Get-Command
C. Get-Member
D. Get-Verb

193. How do you filter commands by their noun in PowerShell?
A. Get-Command -Verb <noun>
B. Get-Command -Noun <string>
C. Get-Command -Noun alias*
D. Get-Command -Filter <noun>

194. What does the Get-Verb cmdlet do?
A. Lists all available verbs in PowerShell.
B. Lists all available nouns in PowerShell.
C. Provides detailed help information about a specific cmdlet.
D. Displays the properties and methods of objects.

195. What is the primary purpose of the Get-Help cmdlet?
A. To list all available commands.
B. To provide help documentation for cmdlets.

C. To display the properties and methods of objects.

D. To add a resource to a container.

196. Which cmdlet would you use to find more information about the properties and methods of an object returned by a command?

A. Get-Command

B. Get-Help

C. Get-Member

D. Get-Verb

197. To see all cmdlets that start with the verb "Add", which flag can you use with Get-Command?

A. -Noun

B. -Verb

C. -Filter

D. -Action

198. What is the recommended tool for authoring and running PowerShell scripts?

A. Notepad

B. PowerShell ISE

C. Visual Studio Code with the PowerShell extension

D. Command Prompt

199. What command would you use to paginate the response of the Get-Help cmdlet for a better reading experience?

A. help <cmdlet> | more

B. Get-Help <cmdlet> -Full

C. Get-Help <cmdlet> -Detailed

D. help <cmdlet> -Online

200. What is the primary purpose of using flags like -Verb and -Noun with the Get-Command cmdlet?

A. To execute commands automatically.

B. To filter the list of available commands based on their verb or noun.

C. To display the help documentation.

D. To update the list of available commands.

201. What is one of the main benefits of using Azure Resource Manager templates?
A. They make deployments faster and more repeatable.
B. They only support single resource deployments.
C. They require manual intervention for each resource.
D. They are not version controllable.

202. Which of the following is a key characteristic of Resource Manager templates?
A. They cannot be versioned.
B. They are written in XML.
C. They use JSON to define resources.
D. They do not support parameters.

203. What is the purpose of the "$schema" element in a Resource Manager template?
A. To provide the version of the template.
B. To define the location of the JSON schema file.
C. To list the resources to be deployed.
D. To specify the parameters for the deployment.

204. How do Resource Manager templates help ensure the correct order of resource deployment?
A. By using manual scripts.
B. By mapping out resources and their dependencies.
C. By requiring user intervention for each step.
D. By deploying all resources simultaneously without regard to dependencies

205. What is the role of the "parameters" section in a Resource Manager template?
A. To define the version of the template.
B. To specify the resources to be deployed.
C. To provide customizable values for the deployment.

D. To return values after deployment.

206. Which element in a Resource Manager template is required and lists the resources to be deployed?
A. parameters
B. variables
C. functions
D. resources

207. What is one way that Resource Manager templates promote reuse?
A. By storing all data in a single template.
B. By allowing templates to be linked together.
C. By requiring manual adjustments for each deployment.
D. By using proprietary formats.

208. What does the "outputs" section in a Resource Manager template do?
A. It defines the location of the JSON schema file.
B. It specifies the version of the template.
C. It returns values after deployment.
D. It lists the variables used in the template.

209. Why is it beneficial to maintain Resource Manager templates under revision control like GIT?
A. To avoid using parameters.
B. To ensure that templates are never changed.
C. To maintain a history of changes and document the deployment evolution.
D. To prevent the use of JSON.

210. What is the advantage of using template parameters in Resource Manager templates?
A. To avoid using JSON.
B. To ensure that the deployment is always the same.
C. To create multiple versions of infrastructure using the same template.
D. To manually adjust each deployment step.

211. What is the maximum number of parameters allowed in an ARM template?
A. 128
B. 256
C. 512
D. 1024

212. Which property of a parameter is used to specify the type of value it can hold?
A. type
B. defaultValue
C. allowed values
D. metadata

213. What is the purpose of the "allowed values" property in a parameter?
A. To set a default value for the parameter
B. To describe the parameter
C. To define the permissible values for the parameter
D. To determine the data type of the parameter

214. Which of the following is NOT a benefit of using Bicep over JSON for template authoring?
A. Simpler syntax
B. Modules for easier management
C. Automatic dependency management
D. Ability to deploy more than 256 parameters

215. How does the Bicep handle dependencies between resources in most situations?
A. Manually through user-defined functions
B. Automatically detects dependencies
C. Requires explicit dependency declaration
D. Dependencies are not managed

216. What is the process called when Bicep converts its template into a JSON template?

A. Compilation
B. Interpretation
C. Transpilation
D. Emulation

217. Which feature of Bicep provides rich validation and IntelliSense for Azure resource type API definitions?
A. Bicep CLI
B. Bicep extension for Visual Studio Code
C. Bicep modules
D. Bicep transpiler

218. What type of parameter should you use for sensitive information like passwords in an ARM template?
A. string
B. int
C. securestring
D. bool

219. In the context of ARM templates, what does the "defaultValue" property specify?
A. The minimum value allowed for the parameter
B. The maximum value allowed for the parameter
C. The default value to be used if no other value is provided
D. The description of the parameter

220. What is one advantage of using string interpolation in Bicep over concatenation in JSON?
A. It increases the execution speed of the template
B. It reduces the template size
C. It simplifies combining values for names and other items
D. It allows for more complex expressions

221. Which Azure storage service is optimized for storing large amounts of unstructured data like documents and media files?
A. Azure Blob Storage

B. Azure Files
C. Azure Queue Storage
D. Azure Table Storage

222. To automate the deployment and configuration of Azure virtual machines (VMs), which Azure service should you use?
A. Azure App Service
B. Azure Automation
C. Azure Container Instances
D. Azure Functions

223. Which Azure service is used to connect an Azure virtual network to an on-premises network securely?
A. Azure Traffic Manager
B. Azure ExpressRoute
C. Azure Load Balancer
D. Azure Virtual WAN

224. What Azure service allows you to collect and analyze data generated by resources in Azure?
A. Azure Monitor
B. Azure Log Analytics
C. Azure Application Insights
D. Azure Service Health

225. Which Azure service provides backup solutions for Azure VMs, Azure Files, and SQL databases?
A. Azure Site Recovery
B. Azure Backup
C. Azure Disaster Recovery
D. Azure Storage Explorer

226. What Azure service allows you to store and manage application secrets, encryption keys, and certificates?
A. Microsoft Defender for Cloud
B. Azure Policy

C. Azure Key Vault

D. Azure Information Protection

227. Which Azure service is used to host domain names and manage DNS records?

A. Azure Traffic Manager

B. Azure DNS

C. Azure Front Door

D. Azure CDN

228. Which Azure role allows users to manage all aspects of Azure subscriptions except access to billing?

A. Owner

B. Contributor

C. Reader

D. User Access Administrator

229. Which feature of Azure virtual machines allows you to automatically adjust the number of VM instances based on demand?

A. Azure Availability Sets

B. Azure Reserved Instances

C. Azure Virtual Machine Scale Sets

D. Azure Hybrid Benefit

230. How can you encrypt data at rest in Azure Blob Storage?

A. Use Azure Storage Service Encryption (SSE)

B. Use Azure Key Vault

C. Use Entra ID authentication

D. Use Azure Information Protection

231. Which Azure service allows you to deploy and manage web applications without managing the underlying infrastructure?

A. Azure Functions

B. Azure App Service

C. Azure Container Instances

D. Azure Kubernetes Service (AKS)

232. Which Azure service distributes incoming traffic across multiple VMs to ensure high availability and reliability?
A. Azure Traffic Manager
B. Azure Application Gateway
C. Azure Load Balancer
D. Azure Front Door

233. What does Azure Policy allow you to enforce in your Azure environment?
A. Network security rules
B. Data encryption standards
C. Compliance with regulatory requirements
D. Resource tagging requirements

234. Which Azure service provides advanced analytics and insights into the performance and health of your Azure resources?
A. Azure Monitor
B. Azure Log Analytics
C. Azure Application Insights
D. Microsoft Defender for Cloud

235. What does Azure Site Recovery help you achieve?
A. High availability for Azure VMs
B. Disaster recovery for on-premises VMs and Azure VMs
C. Data backup for Azure Storage
D. Traffic management for Azure services

236. Which Azure service helps you prevent, detect, and respond to security threats across your Azure environment?
A. Azure Policy
B. Azure Key Vault
C. Microsoft Defender for Cloud
D. Entra ID Identity Protection

237. How does Azure ExpressRoute enhance connectivity to Azure?

A. By providing secure, high-speed connections between Azure data centers and on-premises networks
B. By optimizing data transfer within Azure between different Azure services
C. By managing and monitoring traffic between Azure virtual networks
D. By enabling direct access to Azure services from the internet

238. Which Azure Blob Storage tier offers the lowest storage costs but has higher data retrieval costs?
A. Hot
B. Cool
C. Archive
D. Premium

239. What do Azure Availability Sets ensure for VMs deployed within it?
A. Data encryption at rest
B. High availability and fault tolerance
C. Automatic scaling based on demand
D. Load balancing across multiple VM instances

240. What does Azure Virtual Network peering allow you to do?
A. Connect virtual networks within the same region
B. Connect virtual networks across different Azure regions
C. Connect on-premises networks to Azure virtual networks
D. Establish secure VPN connections to Azure

241. Which Azure service allows you to configure alerts based on metrics, events, and logs generated by Azure resources?
A. Azure Application Insights
B. Microsoft Defender for Cloud
C. Azure Monitor
D. Azure Log Analytics

242. What is the primary use of Azure Site Recovery?
A. Real-time monitoring of Azure resources
B. Data backup and archival

C. Disaster recovery for on-premises and Azure VMs

D. Load balancing across Azure regions

243. How does Azure Key Vault manage access to stored secrets and keys?

A. Through Entra ID authentication

B. By allowing anonymous access

C. By using role-based access control (RBAC)

D. By encrypting access tokens

244. What does Azure Traffic Manager allow you to do?

A. Load balance traffic across multiple Azure VMs within the same region

B. Distribute traffic across multiple Azure regions based on latency or geographic location

C. Manage network security groups (NSGs) for Azure virtual networks

D. Monitor performance metrics of Azure virtual machines

245. What security enhancement does Entra ID Multi-Factor Authentication (MFA) provide?

A. Single sign-on (SSO) for cloud applications

B. Enhanced encryption for Azure storage

C. Additional verification step for user sign-ins

D. Role-based access control (RBAC) for Azure resources

246. Which Azure service provides application-level (Layer 7) load balancing and SSL termination capabilities?

A. Azure Traffic Manager

B. Azure Load Balancer

C. Azure Application Gateway

D. Azure Front Door

247. What does Azure Functions allow you to do?

A. Deploy and manage containerized applications

B. Automate business processes and workflows

C. Create and manage virtual machines

D. Monitor and analyze application performance

248. What is the primary benefit of using Azure Content Delivery Network (CDN)?

A. Enhanced security for Azure services

B. Accelerated delivery of high-bandwidth content to users

C. Load balancing across Azure data centers

D. Real-time monitoring of Azure resources

249. What benefit do Azure Reserved Instances provide?

A. Pay-as-you-go pricing with no upfront costs

B. Flexible scaling of Azure virtual machines based on demand

C. Significant cost savings for long-term workload commitments

D. Automatic backup and recovery of Azure resources

250. Which Azure service provides a fully managed relational database service?

A. Azure Cosmos DB

B. Azure SQL Database

C. Azure Storage

D. Azure Data Lake Storage

251. How does Azure DevOps enhance application lifecycle management?

A. By providing cloud-based IDE for code development

B. By enabling continuous integration and delivery (CI/CD) pipelines

C. By automating deployment and scaling of Azure resources

D. By monitoring application performance and usage metrics

252. What is the primary purpose of Azure Network Security Groups (NSGs)?

A. Load balancing traffic across Azure resources

B. Filtering network traffic to and from Azure resources

C. Monitoring performance metrics of Azure virtual machines

D. Encrypting data at rest in Azure storage

253. What does Azure Kubernetes Service (AKS) provide?

A. Serverless execution environment for containerized applications

B. Managed Kubernetes orchestration service

C. Deployment and management of virtual machine scale sets

D. Integration with Entra ID for identity management

254. What is the primary purpose of Azure Logic Apps?

A. Host and manage serverless APIs

B. Automate workflows and integrate systems

C. Manage and monitor Azure virtual machines

D. Analyze and visualize data insights

255. Which Azure storage service is best suited for storing large amounts of unstructured data with rapid, unpredictable growth and low access frequency?

A. Azure Blob Storage

B. Azure Data Lake Storage Gen2

C. Azure File Storage

D. Azure Disk Storage

256. What is the primary purpose of Azure Bastion?

A. Load balancing traffic across Azure VM instances

B. Securely connect to Azure VMs over RDP and SSH without exposing public IP addresses

C. Monitor and analyze network traffic within Azure virtual networks

D. Provide managed DNS services for Azure resources

257. What is the primary purpose of Azure Resource Groups?

A. Manage Azure subscriptions

B. Organize and manage related Azure resources

C. Monitor network traffic within Azure virtual networks

D. Backup and restore Azure virtual machines

258. What does an Azure App Service Plan define?

A. Network security rules for Azure virtual networks

B. Billing and pricing model for Azure resources

C. Scaling and hosting characteristics for Azure web apps

D. Backup and recovery strategy for Azure SQL databases

259. Which Azure virtual machine disk type offers the lowest latency and highest performance?
A. Standard HDD
B. Standard SSD
C. Premium SSD
D. Ultra Disk

260. What does Azure Backup retention policy determine?
A. Number of VM instances to back up
B. Duration for which backup data is retained
C. Encryption method for backup data
D. Frequency of backup schedule

261. Which deployment model provides a fully managed instance of SQL Server in Azure?
A. Azure SQL Database
B. Azure SQL Managed Instance
C. Azure Cosmos DB
D. Azure SQL Data Warehouse

262. What routing method does Azure Traffic Manager use to distribute user traffic?
A. Round-robin
B. Least connections
C. Priority
D. All of the above

263. Which Azure Storage replication option provides the highest durability and availability?
A. Locally-redundant storage (LRS)
B. Zone-redundant storage (ZRS)
C. Geo-redundant storage (GRS)
D. Read-access geo-redundant storage (RA-GRS)

264. What are common triggers for Azure Functions?
A. HTTP requests, Azure Blob Storage events, and timer-based schedules

B. Virtual machine scaling events and DNS changes

C. Database schema updates and API gateway requests

D. Network security group (NSG) rule changes and SSH connections

265. You need to implement a highly available and scalable Azure solution to host a web application that experiences unpredictable traffic spikes. Which Azure service should be used as the primary compute resource?
A. Azure App Service
B. Azure Virtual Machines
C. Azure Kubernetes Service (AKS)
D. Azure Functions

266. What does Azure Policy enforce in an Azure environment?
A. Performance metrics for Azure resources
B. Compliance with organizational standards and regulatory requirements
C. Encryption methods for Azure storage accounts
D. Network traffic rules for Azure virtual networks

267. What is the primary use case for Azure Container Instances (ACI)?
A. Long-running container orchestrations
B. Batch processing of data workloads
C. Serverless container deployments
D. Hybrid cloud connectivity

268. What does an Azure Policy definition specify?
A. Resource group quotas and limits
B. Access control rules for Azure resources
C. Configuration requirements for Azure resources
D. Billing and cost management guidelines

269. Which Azure virtual network gateway type supports site-to-site VPN connections?
A. VPN Gateway
B. ExpressRoute Gateway
C. Application Gateway
D. Traffic Manager Gateway

270. You need to implement a highly available and scalable Azure solution to process and analyze large volumes of real-time streaming data. Which Azure service should be the core component of your solution?
A. Azure Data Factory
B. Azure Synapse Analytics
C. Azure Stream Analytics
D. Azure Databricks

271. What type of recommendations does Microsoft Defender for Cloud provide?
A. Cost optimization suggestions for Azure resources
B. Performance tuning recommendations for Azure virtual machines
C. Security best practices and remediation steps
D. Network traffic analysis and anomaly detection

272. Which replication scenario does Azure Site Recovery support?
A. Azure VM to on-premises VM
B. Azure VM to Azure VM
C. Azure VM to Azure SQL Database
D. On-premises physical server to Azure Blob Storage

273. What security feature does Azure Bastion provide for connecting to Azure VMs?
A. VPN tunnel encryption
B. Remote Desktop Protocol (RDP) session recording
C. Secure Socket Layer/Transport Layer Security (SSL/TLS) tunneling
D. Network isolation through a private IP address

274. What do Azure Service Health alerts notify you about?
A. Changes in Azure subscription costs
B. Planned maintenance and service incidents affecting your resources
C. Unauthorized access attempts to Azure resources
D. Performance degradation of Azure virtual machines

275. You have an Azure Virtual Network (VNet) with multiple subnets. You need to implement network security groups (NSGs) to control inbound and outbound traffic for specific subnets. Which NSG configuration is most efficient and secure?
A. Apply NSGs to individual virtual machines.
B. Apply NSGs to subnet interfaces.
C. Create network security groups at the VNet level.
D. Use Azure Firewall for all network security.

276. What is the primary purpose of Azure DevOps pipelines?
A. Monitor application performance and usage metrics
B. Manage and version control source code repositories
C. Automate continuous integration and delivery (CI/CD) workflows
D. Provision and manage Azure virtual machines

277. You need to enforce a policy that ensures all Azure resources deployed in your subscription have tags applied with specific metadata. Which Azure service should you use?
A. Azure Policy
B. Azure Resource Locks
C. Azure Blueprint
D. Azure Management Groups

278. You are designing a microservices architecture that requires automated scaling based on CPU utilization and integration with Entra ID for authentication. Which Azure service should you use?
A. Azure Container Instances (ACI)
B. Azure Kubernetes Service (AKS)
C. Azure Service Fabric
D. Azure Functions

279. Your company has multiple branch offices worldwide that need to securely connect to Azure and each other over a private network. Which Azure service should you recommend?
A. Azure Virtual Network
B. Azure Virtual WAN

C. Azure ExpressRoute

D. Azure VPN Gateway

280. You need to orchestrate and automate data movement and transformation workflows between multiple Azure and on-premises data sources. Which Azure service should you use?

A. Azure Databricks

B. Azure Data Factory

C. Azure Synapse Analytics

D. Azure Data Lake Storage

281. You are tasked with implementing disaster recovery for on-premises virtual machines running critical workloads to Azure. Which Azure service or feature should you use?

A. Azure Backup

B. Azure Site Recovery (ASR)

C. Azure Monitor

D. Azure ExpressRoute

282. You need to configure Azure Firewall to allow outbound traffic to specific IP addresses and deny all other outbound traffic. Which type of rule should you create?

A. Network rule

B. Application rule

C. NAT rule

D. Default rule

283. You want to ensure data at rest in Azure Blob Storage is encrypted using customer-managed keys stored in Azure Key Vault. Which encryption option should you choose?

A. Azure Blob Storage encryption

B. Azure Disk Encryption

C. Azure Storage Service Encryption (SSE)

D. Azure Key Vault Encryption

284. You are building a CI/CD pipeline in Azure DevOps for a .NET Core application. Which task should you use to build the application and publish artifacts?
A. Azure CLI task
B. Bash task
C. .NET Core task
D. Build task

285. You need to scale Azure SQL Database to handle increased read-heavy workloads while minimizing cost. Which scaling option should you recommend?
A. Vertical scaling (increasing database DTU or vCore)
B. Horizontal scaling (sharding database across multiple servers)
C. Read-scale-out using read replicas
D. Adding more storage to the database

286. You want to enforce granular network traffic filtering for Azure virtual machines based on specific source IP addresses and ports. Which type of NSG rule should you configure?
A. Inbound security rule
B. Outbound security rule
C. Application security rule
D. Service endpoint rule

287. You have two Azure virtual networks (VNet-A and VNet-B) deployed in the same Azure region. VNet-A is connected to an on-premises network via Azure ExpressRoute. You need VMs in VNet-B to communicate securely with on-premises resources through VNet-A without transiting over the public internet. What should you configure?
A. Virtual network gateway
B. Virtual network peering
C. Azure Private Link
D. Azure Bastion

288. You need to implement an Azure solution to monitor and analyze log data from multiple Azure resources. Which Azure service is best suited for centralizing and analyzing this log data?
A. Azure Monitor
B. Azure Data Factory
C. Azure Event Hubs
D. Azure Log Analytics

289. You need to grant an Azure service (such as Azure SQL Database) access to secrets stored in Azure Key Vault without exposing sensitive credentials. Which Key Vault feature should you use?
A. Azure Key Vault Managed HSM
B. Azure Key Vault Access Policies
C. Azure Key Vault Soft Delete
D. Azure Key Vault RBAC

290. You are designing a highly available application architecture in Azure that requires load-balancing traffic between multiple VM instances in the same Azure region. Which type of Azure Load Balancer should you use?
A. Public Load Balancer
B. Internal Load Balancer
C. Application Gateway
D. Traffic Manager

291. Your organization needs to enforce a set of Azure policies across multiple Azure subscriptions and management groups. Which Azure service should you use to group and enforce these policies collectively?
A. Azure Policy Assignments
B. Azure Policy Definitions
C. Azure Policy Initiative
D. Azure Policy Compliance

292. You are deploying a Kubernetes cluster in Azure that needs to pull Docker container images securely from Azure Container Registry (ACR). Which authentication method should you configure for the Kubernetes cluster?

A. Managed identities for Azure resources
B. Service principal with a password
C. Service principal with a certificate
D. OAuth token authentication

293. You want to implement disaster recovery for the Azure SQL Database by replicating data to another Azure region for high availability. Which type of Azure SQL Database replication should you configure?
A. Active geo-replication
B. Zone-redundant database
C. Geo-redundant database
D. Read-scale-out replica

294. You are designing a global application deployment in Azure that requires routing user traffic to the nearest datacenter based on geographic proximity. Which routing method should you configure in Azure Traffic Manager?
A. Weighted routing
B. Geographic routing
C. Priority routing
D. Performance routing

295. You are developing an Azure Functions app that exposes HTTP-triggered endpoints and needs to enforce authentication and authorization using Entra ID identities. Which feature should you configure?
A. Entra ID application registration
B. Azure API Management
C. Azure Functions Authentication/Authorization feature
D. Azure App Service Authentication/Authorization feature

296. You are designing a data storage solution in Azure that requires cost-effective storage for data accessed infrequently with flexible latency requirements. Which Azure Storage access tier should you recommend?
A. Hot access tier
B. Cool access tier
C. Archive access tier

D. Premium access tier

297. What is the primary function of Azure Resource Manager (ARM) in Microsoft Azure?
A. To manage Azure subscriptions and billing
B. To deploy, manage, and organize Azure resources
C. To monitor Azure resource performance
D. To provide networking services within Azure

298. Which Azure service is suitable for scalable cloud storage with access tier options like Hot, Cool, and Archive?
A. Azure Files
B. Azure Blob storage
C. Azure Table storage
D. Azure Queue storage

299. Which Azure service provides a managed platform for building, deploying, and scaling web applications?
A. Azure Kubernetes Service (AKS)
B. Azure Functions
C. Azure App Services
D. Azure Container Instances

300. Which Azure networking service provides a scalable solution for load balancing HTTP/HTTPS traffic and SSL offloading?
A. Azure Traffic Manager
B. Azure Front Door
C. Azure Application Gateway
D. Azure Load Balancer

301. Which of the following is not a core concept of Azure Role-Based Access Control (RBAC)?
A. Security principal
B. Role definition
C. Scope
D. Load balancer

302. What role should you assign to a user who needs full access to manage all resources, including the ability to assign roles in Azure RBAC?
A. Reader
B. Contributor
C. Owner
D. User Access Administrator

303. When defining a custom role in Azure RBAC, which permission set specifies what actions are not allowed?
A. Actions
B. NotActions
C. DataActions
D. AssignableScopes

304. Which of the following practices can help in maintaining security while implementing roles and scope assignments in Azure RBAC?
A. Assigning all users as Owners
B. Using built-in roles exclusively
C. Limiting access scope to the minimum required for job duties
D. Allowing data modifications without restrictions

305. What is the primary purpose of a role assignment in Azure?
A. To increase system performance
B. To control access
C. To manage billing
D. To enable multi-factor authentication

306. Which role in Azure RBAC can create and manage all types of Azure resources but cannot grant access to others?
A. Owner
B. Contributor
C. Reader
D. User Access Administrator

307. In Microsoft Entra ID, what is the most restricted type of user account?
A. Administrator
B. Member
C. Guest
D. Global Administrator

308. Which command would you use in Azure PowerShell to create a new user?
A. az ad user create
B. New-MgUser
C. New-AzUser
D. Add-AzureUser

309. What is the primary benefit of using Microsoft Entra B2B for collaboration with external partners?
A. Simplified access management without the need for managing external users' identities
B. Requirement for external users to have an IT department
C. Necessity to establish a federation and trust
D. Dependency on an on-premises server for authentication

310. Which type of access assignment automatically manages group membership based on user or device properties?
A. Direct assignment
B. Group assignment
C. Role-based access control (RBAC)
D. Rule-based assignment

311. What feature allows employees to manage their Azure subscriptions using their existing work identities?
A. Azure role-based access control (Azure RBAC)
B. Microsoft Entra Connect
C. Azure Resource Manager
D. Direct assignment

312. Which of the following is not a scenario you can implement with Azure RBAC?
A. Allowing a user to manage all resources in a resource group
B. Allowing external users to manage Azure resources without an invitation
C. Allowing a database administrator group to manage SQL databases in a subscription
D. Allowing an application to access all resources in a resource group

313. What is a "security principal" in the context of Azure RBAC?
A. A collection of permissions
B. A user, group, or application granted access
C. The level where access applies
D. The process of binding a role to a security principal

314. Which built-in role in Azure RBAC allows full access to all resources and the ability to delegate access to others?
A. Contributor
B. Reader
C. Owner
D. User Access Administrator

315. What does the scope in Azure RBAC determine?
A. The permissions that the role can perform
B. The types of Azure resources that can be managed
C. The level where the access applies
D. The process of granting and revoking access

316. In Azure RBAC, what is the purpose of 'NotActions' permissions?
A. To create a new role assignment
B. To define the level of access for a security principal
C. To create a set of not allowed permissions
D. To list the operations that a role can perform

317. What is the primary benefit of using Self-Service Password Reset (SSPR) in Microsoft Entra ID?
A. Increased administrative workload

B. Reduced help-desk costs

C. Limited user access to password reset options

D. Reduced user productivity

318. Which of the following is not an authentication method supported by SSPR in Microsoft Entra ID?
A. Mobile app notification
B. Fingerprint scan
C. Security questions
D. Email

319. What is the minimum number of authentication methods that can be specified for users to register in SSPR?
A. One
B. Two
C. Three
D. Four

320. Which Microsoft Entra ID editions support self-service password reset if the user is not signed in and has forgotten their password?
A. Free edition only
B. Premium P1 and P2 only
C. All editions
D. Premium P1, P2, and Microsoft 365 Apps for business

321. What type of data does Azure Blob Storage handle?
A. Structured data
B. Unstructured data
C. Virtual machine data
D. Relational data

322. Which service is a fully managed file share in Azure?
A. Azure Blob Storage
B. Azure Table Storage
C. Azure File Storage
D. Azure Data Lake Storage

323. What type of storage account should be used for I/O-intensive applications like databases?
A. Standard tier storage account
B. Basic tier storage account
C. Premium tier storage account
D. Low-latency tier storage account

324. Which type of data is stored in a relational format with a shared schema?
A. Unstructured data
B. Semi-structured data
C. Virtual machine data
D. Structured data

325. What service is used for massively scalable object storage in Azure?
A. Azure Queue Storage
B. Azure Blob Storage
C. Azure File Storage
D. Azure Disk Storage

326. Which storage option is used for a NoSQL store in Azure?
A. Azure Blob Storage
B. Azure Table Storage
C. Azure File Storage
D. Azure Queue Storage

327. What type of data does Azure Data Lake Storage handle?
A. Structured data
B. Unstructured data
C. Virtual machine data
D. Relational data

328. Which of the following is not a feature of Azure Storage?
A. Durability and high availability
B. Secure access with encryption

C. Limited scalability

D. Manageability with automatic maintenance

329. What is the maximum capacity of each data disk used by Azure virtual machines?
A. 1,024 GB
B. 16,384 GB
C. 32,767 GB
D. 64,000 GB

330. How does Azure Storage ensure data accessibility?
A. Data is only accessible within the same region
B. Data is accessible from anywhere in the world over HTTP or HTTPS.
C. Data requires a dedicated network connection.
D. Data is only accessible through the Azure portal.

331. Which Azure Storage service is optimized for storing massive amounts of unstructured data?
A. Azure Files
B. Azure Queue Storage
C. Azure Table Storage
D. Azure Blob Storage

332. Which protocol can be used to access Azure Files?
A. HTTP
B. FTP
C. SMB
D. SCP

333. What is the maximum size of a message that can be stored in Azure Queue Storage?
A. 16 KB
B. 32 KB
C. 64 KB
D. 128 KB

334. Which Azure Storage service is best suited for storing non-relational structured data?
A. Azure Blob Storage
B. Azure Files
C. Azure Queue Storage
D. Azure Table Storage

335. Which Azure Storage service allows for the creation of highly available network file shares?
A. Azure Blob Storage
B. Azure Files
C. Azure Queue Storage
D. Azure Table Storage

336. Which of the following can access objects in Azure Blob Storage?
A. URLs
B. Azure PowerShell
C. Azure CLI
D. All of the above

337. What is a common use case for Azure Queue Storage?
A. Storing diagnostic logs
B. Serving images to a browser
C. Creating a backlog of work to process asynchronously
D. Storing configuration files

338. Which Azure Storage service is most cost-effective for many types of applications compared to traditional SQL?
A. Azure Blob Storage
B. Azure Files
C. Azure Queue Storage
D. Azure Table Storage

339. Which of the following is a best practice when managing access keys in Azure Storage?
A. Use a single access key for all applications and services.

B. Regularly rotate access keys and regenerate them as needed.

C. Share access keys with third-party applications.

D. Disable the access keys permanently after use.

340. How can Azure Files simplify the migration of on-premises applications to Azure?

A. By using the same drive letter that the on-premises application uses

B. By providing access through FTP

C. By integrating with Azure Table Storage

D. By compressing the files before migration

341. What is the primary benefit of using Azure Virtual Machine Scale Sets?

A. They allow for manual management of network configurations.

B. They provide a way to deploy and manage a set of identical virtual machines with true autoscaling.

C. They support up to 600 virtual machine instances using base operating system images.

D. They increase security by isolating each virtual machine instance.

342. Which of the following is true about the traffic distribution capabilities supported by Azure Virtual Machine Scale Sets?

A. They only support Azure Load Balancer for traffic distribution.

B. They support Azure Application Gateway for layer-4 traffic distribution and SSL termination.

C. They support both Azure Load Balancer for layer-4 traffic distribution and Azure Application Gateway for layer-7 traffic distribution and SSL termination.

D. They do not support any form of traffic distribution.

343. What is the maximum number of virtual machine instances supported by Azure Virtual Machine Scale Sets when using custom virtual machine images?

A. 500 virtual machine instances

B. 600 virtual machine instances

C. 800 virtual machine instances

D. 1,000 virtual machine instances

344. What is the primary difference between flexible and uniform orchestration modes in Azure Virtual Machine Scale Sets?
A. Flexible mode allows for automatic scaling, while uniform mode requires manual scaling.
B. Flexible mode allows manual creation of VMs with different configurations, while uniform mode creates identical VMs based on a defined model.
C. Flexible mode supports only x64 architecture, while uniform mode supports both x64 and Arm64 architectures.
D. Flexible mode is costlier compared to uniform mode.

345. What is the benefit of using Azure Spot instances in Virtual Machine Scale Sets?
A. Guaranteed availability of resources.
B. Discounted rates compared to pay-as-you-go prices.
C. Higher performance compared to standard instances.
D. Longer uptime and stability.

346. If you need to scale your Virtual Machine Scale Sets implementation beyond 100 instances, which setting should you configure?
A. VM Architecture
B. Orchestration mode
C. Enable scaling beyond 100 instances
D. Size

347. What is the primary purpose of autoscaling in an Azure Virtual Machine Scale Sets implementation?
A. To maintain a fixed number of virtual machines.
B. To dynamically adjust the number of virtual machines to meet changing workload demands.
C. To manually increase the number of virtual machines during high demand.
D. To ensure the application always runs on a maximum number of virtual machines.

348. Which of the following settings in the Azure portal is used to specify the CPU usage percentage threshold to trigger a scale-out autoscale rule?
A. Minimum number of VMs
B. Maximum number of VMs
C. Scale-out CPU threshold
D. Scale in CPU threshold

349. What should you consider when configuring the 'duration in minutes' setting for autoscaling?
A. The maximum number of virtual machines in the implementation.
B. The minimum number of virtual machines in the implementation.
C. The amount of time the autoscale engine will look back for metrics to avoid reacting to transient spikes.
D. The number of virtual machines to increase by.

350. What type of solutions does Azure Backup provide?
A. Complex, secure, and expensive
B. Simple, secure, and cost-effective
C. Simple, insecure, and cost-effective
D. Complex, insecure, and free

351. Which of the following is not a workload that Azure Backup can protect?
A. Azure Virtual Machines
B. SQL and SAP databases
C. Azure file shares
D. Google Cloud Storage

352. What is a key feature of the Azure Backup service's management interface?
A. It is decentralized and difficult to use
B. It requires a lot of infrastructure to manage
C. It makes it easy to define backup policies
D. It is only accessible via the command line

353. Which of the following best describes Azure Backup's infrastructure requirements?
A. High-infrastructure
B. Zero-infrastructure
C. Medium-infrastructure
D. Custom-infrastructure

354. What type of workloads can Azure Backup protect?
A. On-premises files and folders
B. Azure Virtual Machines (VMs)
C. SQL Server in Azure VMs
D. All of the above

355. Which of the following tools would you use to prepare your data for an Azure Import/Export job?
A. Azure Storage Explorer
B. Azure Import/Export tool
C. Azure Data Factory
D. Azure Backup

356. What is the purpose of the Backup Center in Azure Backup?
A. To manage encryption settings
B. To automate storage expansion
C. To centrally manage the entire backup estate
D. To configure private endpoints

357. If your organization has an RPO of one hour and an RTO of three hours for a customer database, what does this mean?
A. Backups are performed every three hours, and the system must be restored within one hour.
B. Backups are performed every hour, and the system must be restored within three hours.
C. The system must be restored within one hour and backups are taken every three hours.
D. The system must be restored within three hours and backups are taken every three hours.

358. What is the primary purpose of the Azure Backup service?
A. To provide real-time data processing
B. To offer a platform for deploying applications
C. To back up data, machine state, and workloads running on on-premises machines and VM instances to the Azure cloud
D. To manage network security and firewalls

359. Which of the following backup types does Azure Backup support?
A. Full backups and differential backups only
B. Full backups, incremental backups, and SQL Server backups
C. Incremental backups and hourly backups only
D. Only full backups

360. What is the role of a vault in Azure Backup?
A. It acts as a firewall for network security
B. It provides an interface for deploying applications
C. It is an online-storage entity used to hold data such as backup copies, recovery points, and backup policies
D. It manages real-time data processing

361. Which feature allows you to back up only a subset of data disks attached to your VM in Azure Backup?
A. Full Disk Backup
B. Selective Disk Backup
C. Incremental Disk Backup
D. Comprehensive Disk Backup

362. What is the primary advantage of using the Snapshot tier for VM backups?
A. Lower cost compared to other tiers
B. Faster restore times
C. Higher redundancy
D. Longer retention period

363. Which of the following storage tiers is specifically designed for long-term retention (LTR) backup data?
A. Snapshot tier
B. Vault-Standard tier
C. Archive tier
D. Premium tier

364. What feature does Azure Backup provide to protect against malicious deletion of your backup data?
A. Immutable storage
B. Soft-delete operations
C. Data masking
D. Multi-factor authentication

365. Which component in Azure Backup provides an interface for users to interact with the backup service and manage backup policies?
A. Recovery Services vault/Backup vault
B. Azure Blob storage
C. Azure Key Vault
D. Azure Monitor

366. Which replication option would you choose if you want to ensure that data is replicated synchronously within a single region but across different availability zones?
A. Locally Redundant Storage (LRS)
B. Zone-Redundant Storage (ZRS)
C. Geo-Redundant Storage (GRS)
D. Read-Access Geo-Redundant Storage (RA-GRS)

367. Which alert type in Azure Monitor would you use to get notified when an Azure resource changes state?
A. Metric alert
B. Log alert
C. Activity log alert
D. Health alert

368. What are the severity levels available for alerts in Azure Monitor?
A. 0: Critical, 1: Major, 2: Minor, 3: Informational, 4: Verbose
B. 0: Critical, 1: Warning, 2: Error, 3: Informational, 4: Verbose
C. 0: Critical, 1: Error, 2: Warning, 3: Informational, 4: Verbose
D. 0: High, 1: Medium, 2: Low, 3: Informational, 4: Verbose

369. In the composition of an alert rule in Azure Monitor, what is an action group typically used for?
A. Defining the alert condition
B. Specifying the resource to monitor
C. Containing a unique set of recipients for the action
D. Setting the severity level of the alert

370. Which type of metric alert would you use if you want to define a specific threshold value for CPU utilization that triggers an alert when the threshold is exceeded?
A. Dynamic threshold metric alert
B. Static threshold metric alert
C. Scaling metric alert
D. Dimension metric alert

371. What additional parameters must be defined when setting up a dynamic threshold metric alert?
A. Evaluation period and notification method
B. Number of violations and look-back period
C. Minimum and maximum thresholds
D. CPU utilization and disk space

372. What is the primary benefit of using dimensions in metric alerts in Azure Monitor?
A. To reduce the number of notifications received
B. To monitor data from multiple target instances with a single alert rule
C. To automatically scale the resources being monitored
D. To ensure alerts are only sent during business hours

373. How does Azure Monitor handle metric alert evaluations for static threshold metric alerts?
A. By using machine-learning algorithms to adjust the thresholds dynamically
B. By assessing data for the last defined period and checking the rule at regular intervals
C. By only sending notifications when multiple conditions are met
D. By evaluating the entire resource group collectively

374. What is the primary nature of log alerts in Azure Monitor?
A. Stateful
B. Stateless
C. Event-driven
D. Predictive

375. Which of the following Azure Storage replication options provides the highest level of durability and availability by replicating data across multiple regions?
A. Locally Redundant Storage (LRS)
B. Zone-Redundant Storage (ZRS)
C. Geo-Redundant Storage (GRS)
D. Read-Access Geo-Redundant Storage (RA-GRS)

376. Which of the following is a component of a log search rule in Azure Monitor?
A. Alert priority
B. Notification method
C. Log query
D. Alert description

377. Which type of activity log alert should you use if you want to be notified when a new role is assigned to a user within your Azure subscription?
A. Metric alerts
B. Log alerts

C. Specific operations

D. Service health events

378. When creating a service health alert, what is the primary difference compared to creating other types of alerts?

A. You need to select a specific resource

B. You need to specify a threshold value

C. You need to select a whole region in Azure

D. You need to set a time interval for monitoring

379. Which attribute of an activity log alert specifies whether the event is informational, a warning, an error, or critical?

A. Category

B. Scope

C. Level

D. Status

380. Which Azure service is specifically designed to transfer large amounts of data to and from Azure using physical disks?

A. Azure File Sync

B. Azure Blob Storage

C. Azure Data Box

D. Azure Import/Export

381. Which of the following is not an action that Azure Monitor can perform through an action group?

A. Send an email.

B. Restart a VM.

C. Create an ITSM ticket.

D. Modify subscription billing.

382. What is the primary purpose of the Azure Import/Export service?

A. To transfer data between different Azure regions

B. To move data between on-premises and Azure using physical drives

C. To replicate data across Azure Storage accounts

D. To monitor data transfer rates in Azure

383. What is the primary purpose of Azure Monitor Metrics for Azure VMs?
A. To store log data for querying and analysis.
B. To measure VM performance and resource utilization.
C. To archive data for long-term storage.
D. To manage the deployment of VMs.

384. Which of the following destinations can activity logs be sent to for more complex querying and alerting?
A. Azure Storage
B. Azure Event Hubs
C. Azure Monitor Logs
D. Azure Monitor Metrics

385. Which of the following is not a metric automatically collected by Azure for VM hosts?
A. CPU usage percentage (average)
B. Network operations (total)
C. Disk operations per second (average)
D. Application error counts

386. What feature of Azure Monitor allows you to plot multiple metrics on a graph and investigate changes visually?
A. Azure Monitor Alerts
B. Azure Monitor Logs
C. Metrics Explorer
D. Boot Diagnostics

387. What is the function of boot diagnostics in Azure VMs?
A. To monitor network operations.
B. To help troubleshoot boot issues.
C. To collect application performance data.
D. To manage resource utilization.

388. What do you need to install on a VM to collect metrics and logs from the guest OS, client workloads, and applications?

A. Azure Monitor Agent
B. Azure Security Center
C. Azure Resource Manager
D. Azure DevOps Agent

389. Where can you store both metrics and event log data collected from a VM?
A. Azure Monitor Metrics
B. Azure Monitor Logs
C. Azure Blob Storage
D. Azure SQL Database

390. What do VM insights provide to simplify monitoring a VM's guest OS and workloads?
A. Predefined application templates
B. Simplified Azure Monitor Agent onboarding
C. Automated backup solutions
D. Integrated development environment

391. Which of the following can be optionally collected by VM insights?
A. CPU usage data
B. Running processes on the VM
C. Network bandwidth statistics
D. Disk space usage

392. What language is used to write log queries for analyzing data stored in a Log Analytics workspace?
A. SQL
B. Python
C. Kusto Query Language (KQL)
D. JavaScript

393. What is the first step to create a new VM in the Azure portal?
A. Select Review + create
B. Enter the VM name

C. Sign in to the Azure portal and search for virtual machines

D. Select Ubuntu Server 20.04 LTS-x64 Gen2

394. Which of the following should be selected for the Image when creating a new VM?

A. Windows Server 2022

B. Ubuntu Server 20.04 LTS-x64 Gen2

C. Red Hat Enterprise Linux

D. CentOS

395. What setting should be enabled under Diagnostics during the VM creation process?

A. Enable guest OS diagnostics

B. Enable with a managed storage account

C. Disable boot diagnostics

D. None of the above

396. Which tab allows you to select the checkbox next to "Enable recommended alert rules"?

A. Basics tab

B. Disks tab

C. Networking tab

D. Monitoring tab

397. Where can you view the activity log of the VM after it has been created?

A. On the VM's Overview page

B. Under the Activity log in the VM's left navigation menu

C. Within the Performance and utilization section

D. On the Boot diagnostics page

398. What is the purpose of installing the Azure Monitor Agent on a VM?

A. To enhance network security

B. To collect data from inside the VM

C. To manage storage solutions

D. To backup VM data

399. What do VM insights create to collect and send client performance data to a Log Analytics workspace?
A. A virtual network
B. A data collection rule (DCR)
C. A storage account
D. A network security group

400. Which agent is recommended to be selected on the Monitoring configuration page when enabling VM insights?
A. Azure Security Agent
B. Azure Backup Agent
C. Azure Monitor Agent
D. Azure Storage Agent

Answers

1. Answer: B

Explanation: Cloud computing involves delivering various computing services such as servers, storage, databases, and software over the internet, enabling on-demand access and pay-as-you-go pricing models.

2. Answer: D

Explanation: The major cloud providers mentioned are Amazon (AWS), Google (Google Cloud Platform), and Microsoft (Azure). Facebook is not listed as a major cloud provider.

3. Answer: C

Explanation: Cloud computing typically uses a pay-as-you-go pricing model, where users pay only for the resources and services they consume. This model allows for flexibility and scalability, as costs are directly tied to usage.

4. Answer: B

Explanation: Cloud computing removes the need for capital expenditure on buying hardware and software, as well as building and running in-house data centers.

5. Answer: B

Explanation: Cloud computing ensures reliability through features like data backup, disaster recovery, and business continuity, making it possible for businesses to maintain critical functions after an emergency.

6. Answer: C

Explanation: The consumption-based model in cloud computing means that users pay only for the resources they consume without the need to invest in and maintain expensive infrastructure.

7. **Answer: C**

Explanation: Auto-scaling automatically deploys additional resources when demand increases and scales down when demand decreases, ensuring consistent performance.

8. **Answer: B**

Explanation: Cloud computing is classified as Operational Expenditure (OpEx) because it involves ongoing expenses for services rather than one-time capital investments.

9. **Answer: C**

Explanation: Cloud providers offer advanced security features to protect data, applications, and infrastructure, enhancing overall security for organizations.

10. **Answer: C**

Explanation: A Virtual Machine (VM) is a software-based compute resource in cloud computing that runs programs and deploys applications, functioning similarly to a physical computer.

11. **Answer: C**

Explanation: The main advantage of SaaS (Software as a Service) is that it enables easy access to cloud-based applications without the need to install hardware and software. This model offers significant benefits, including accessibility from any device with the internet, cost savings on hardware and maintenance, automatic updates, and scalability to meet growing demands, all managed by the service provider.

12. Answer: C

Explanation: IaaS (Infrastructure as a Service) enables businesses to rapidly deploy computing infrastructure without investing in and maintaining physical hardware, making it an ideal solution for organizations requiring flexibility and scalability.

13. Answer: B

Explanation: In SaaS (Software as a Service), the cloud provider manages the infrastructure and applications, but the customer is responsible for the data and information stored in the cloud.

14. Answer: C

Explanation: The Hybrid Cloud model allows organizations to use both on-premises and cloud resources, providing flexibility and scalability according to their needs.

15. Answer: B

Explanation: PaaS (Platform as a Service) provides developers with a platform that includes pre-configured environments, tools, and services, which streamline the development process and significantly reduce deployment time. It allows developers to focus on writing code and creating applications without worrying about the underlying infrastructure, thereby accelerating the development lifecycle.

16. Answer: C

Explanation: In Software as a Service (SaaS), the cloud provider handles most responsibilities, including infrastructure and application management.

The user's primary responsibilities are managing their data and configuring the software for their needs. This setup reduces complexity, saves costs, allows easy scalability, and provides accessible software from any device with internet connectivity.

17. Answer: B

Explanation: Infrastructure as a Service (IaaS) is ideal for high-performance computing (HPC) workloads because it offers powerful virtualized computing resources on demand. This eliminates the need for businesses to invest in and maintain costly physical hardware. With IaaS, organizations can quickly scale up or down based on workload requirements, ensuring they have the necessary processing power when needed. This flexibility and scalability make it a cost-effective and efficient solution for handling intensive computational tasks, such as data analysis, scientific simulations, and complex modeling.

18. Answer: B

Explanation: Platform as a Service (PaaS) enables development teams to collaborate efficiently by providing a unified development environment accessible over the Internet. This shared platform includes tools, libraries, and frameworks that standardize development processes, ensuring consistency and compatibility across different parts of the project. Because PaaS is cloud-based, team members can work from any location, accessing the same resources and development tools. This setup enhances collaboration, as developers can easily share code, track progress, and manage project tasks in real-time, leading to more efficient teamwork and streamlined project management.

19. Answer: B

Explanation: The "pay-as-you-go" model means you only pay for the cloud services and resources you use, enabling cost efficiency and scalability. This approach helps avoid upfront costs and over-provisioning, allowing businesses to scale resources up or down based on demand.

20. **Answer: A**

Explanation: The Public Cloud model is managed by the cloud provider, offering lower costs, scalability, and flexibility, as users only pay for the resources they use without needing to manage physical hardware.

21. **Answer: B**

Explanation: A data center is a physical facility that houses network servers and the necessary infrastructure to support various Azure services. It provides the environment needed for computing resources, such as power, cooling, and security. By hosting servers and related components, data centers enable the delivery of cloud services, including storage, networking, and applications, ensuring reliability and performance for users.

22. **Answer: B**

Explanation: Azure's global regions ensure data residency, compliance, and resilience by strategically locating data centers worldwide. This setup supports high performance, low-latency connectivity, and availability through multiple availability zones, benefiting global applications with secure, compliant, and resilient cloud services.

23. **Answer: B**

Explanation: Azure boasts a global network of 54 regions worldwide, each comprising multiple data centers. This extensive footprint allows users to deploy applications close to their end-users, ensuring low latency, data residency compliance, and high availability through redundant availability zones.

24. **Answer: D**

Explanation: When selecting an Azure region, three primary factors should be considered: location, feature availability, and price. Choosing a region close to your users or operations minimizes latency, resulting in faster response times and an improved user experience. Additionally, not all Azure regions offer the same services, so it's essential to ensure the region you select supports the specific Azure features and services your application requires. Finally, service costs can vary between regions, so it's important to compare pricing to find a region that offers the services you need at a competitive rate.

25. Answer: B

Explanation: An Availability Zone is a distinct physical location within an Azure region, each equipped with its own independent power, cooling, and networking infrastructure. These zones are designed to ensure high availability by providing redundancy and isolation from failures in other zones within the same region. By deploying resources across multiple Availability Zones, businesses can protect their applications and data from localized failures, ensuring continuity and reliability. This setup helps in achieving better fault tolerance, lower latency, and higher resilience for critical applications and services.

26. Answer: B

Explanation: An Azure Region Pair consists of two regions within the same geographic area that are strategically placed far enough apart to ensure that large-scale disasters, such as natural disasters or major outages, do not affect both regions simultaneously. This pairing ensures that in the event of a significant outage in one region, the other region can be prioritized and continue to maintain service availability. Additionally, region pairs provide data residency, replication, and recovery features, enabling seamless failover and continuity of services during planned maintenance or unexpected downtime. This design enhances the reliability and resilience of applications hosted on Azure.

27. Answer: B

Explanation: Data residency refers to the specific physical or geographic location where an organization's data is stored. This concept is critical for ensuring compliance with local laws and regulations regarding data privacy and security. By knowing the exact location of their data, organizations can ensure that they adhere to legal requirements, such as those imposed by data protection laws like the General Data Protection Regulation (GDPR) in the European Union, which may mandate that certain types of data remain within specific geographical boundaries. This helps in safeguarding data, maintaining privacy, and ensuring that the data is managed in accordance with relevant legal and regulatory frameworks.

28. Answer: D

Explanation: An Availability Set is a feature in Azure that helps ensure virtual machines (VMs) are distributed across multiple physical servers within a data center. This distribution minimizes the risk of a single point of failure affecting the availability of your application. By spreading VMs across different physical hardware, an Availability Set provides redundancy, ensuring that in case of hardware or software failures, only a subset of your VMs is impacted, thus maintaining the overall availability and reliability of your services.

29. Answer: C

Explanation: US Gov. Virginia is a specialized Azure region tailored to meet the stringent compliance and security requirements of U.S. government agencies. This region provides enhanced security measures and regulatory compliance, ensuring that sensitive government data is handled according to federal standards. It offers the same robust Azure services as public regions but within a secure environment that meets the unique needs of government operations.

30. Answer: B

Explanation: Failover refers to the capability to automatically and seamlessly switch to a reliable backup system in case of a service disruption.

This ensures continuity of service by redirecting operations to standby resources without manual intervention, minimizing downtime and maintaining operational stability.

31. Answer: C

Explanation: Azure Portal is a web-based, unified console that provides a graphical user interface to interact with Azure services. It is the most common way to build, manage, and monitor resources in Azure. Through Azure Portal, users can create and configure virtual machines, manage storage accounts, deploy web applications, and monitor service health and usage. The portal integrates various Azure services into a single view, simplifying management and operational tasks while providing detailed insights and analytics for resource optimization.

32. Answer: A

Explanation: Azure CLI (Command-Line Interface) is a tool that allows users to manage Azure resources through text-based commands. It is designed for scripting and automation, providing a powerful way to execute operations without the need for a graphical user interface. Users enter commands in a terminal or command prompt to create, modify, and manage Azure services such as virtual machines, databases, and storage accounts. Azure CLI supports both interactive use and automation through scripts, making it a flexible and efficient option for managing Azure environments.

33. Answer: B

Explanation: Azure CLI (Command-Line Interface) is a robust tool designed for interacting with Azure resources through text-based commands. It offers stability and reliability for automation due to its consistent syntax and backward compatibility across versions. Azure CLI commands rarely change once implemented, ensuring scripts remain dependable over time. This stability, coupled with extensive documentation and community support, makes Azure CLI ideal for automating complex workflows, managing deployments, and orchestrating Azure resources effectively in various DevOps environments. Its integration with scripting languages and DevOps tools further enhances its utility for seamless cloud operations and continuous integration and deployment practices.

34. Answer: B

Explanation: Azure PowerShell is a command-line tool designed for managing Azure resources through task-oriented cmdlets. These cmdlets follow a verb-noun naming convention and provide robust capabilities for automating Azure tasks, deploying infrastructure, and configuring resources across Windows, macOS, and Linux platforms. Azure PowerShell integrates seamlessly with Azure services, supports scripting for automation, and maintains stability and backward compatibility across updates, making it a preferred choice for administrators and developers to efficiently manage Azure environments.

35. Answer: C

Explanation: The command "az --version" is essential for verifying the current version of Azure CLI installed on your system. This command provides quick access to information about the Azure CLI version, ensuring compatibility with Azure services and features. It is a fundamental utility for administrators and developers managing Azure resources, enabling them to stay informed about updates and maintain effective operations within their Azure environment.

36. Answer: D

Explanation: Azure Cloud Shell provides a powerful cloud-based command-line interface (CLI) within the Azure portal. It includes an integrated file editor and dedicated storage to persist data between sessions, offering convenience and flexibility for managing Azure resources directly from the browser. This tool eliminates the need for local installations of CLI tools, ensuring consistent access to Azure functionalities across different devices. With built-in support for popular programming languages and

Azure tools, Cloud Shell streamlines administrative tasks and enhances productivity for developers and IT professionals alike.

37. Answer: B

Explanation: The `New-AzVM` command in Azure PowerShell allows users to swiftly create new virtual machines (VMs) in their Azure environment. This cmdlet is essential for provisioning VMs by specifying parameters such as resource group, VM name, region, operating system image, size, and credentials. It simplifies the process of deploying VMs through automation, leveraging PowerShell's scripting capabilities to streamline infrastructure management and accelerate deployment times in Azure.

38. Answer: C

Explanation: Azure CLI is a versatile command-line tool that offers cross-compatibility across major operating systems, including Windows, macOS, and Linux. This allows users to manage Azure resources seamlessly regardless of their preferred platform. Whether executing commands for virtual machines, databases, or storage services, Azure CLI provides a consistent experience across environments, making it accessible and efficient for developers and administrators working in diverse computing environments.

39. Answer: C

Explanation: Azure Portal is the central management interface for Microsoft Azure, offering a unified dashboard to access and manage all Azure services and resources through a web-based platform.

40. Answer: C

Explanation: Azure Portal provides several benefits, including the capability to monitor both current and projected costs associated with Azure resources. This feature allows users to gain insights into their expenditures, helping them manage budgets more effectively and optimize resource usage based on financial forecasts. Additionally, Azure Portal offers cost management tools and reporting functionalities that enable users to track spending patterns, identify cost-saving opportunities, and adjust resource allocations as needed to align with business objectives.

41. **Answer: B**

Explanation: Azure App Service is a PaaS offering that allows you to create and host web apps, mobile back-ends, and RESTful APIs without network maintenance. It supports multiple programming languages and offers high availability and auto-scaling.

42. **Answer: B**

Explanation: The API Gateway in Azure API Management accepts API calls and routes them to the backend. It also offers features such as authorization and caching.

43. **Answer. C**

Explanation: Azure Site Recovery is a service used for business continuity and disaster recovery (DR). It provides failover and failback capabilities, ensuring high availability and built-in DR solutions.

44. **Answer: B**

Explanation: Microsoft Entra ID B2C provides consumer identity and access management for consumer-based applications, allowing users to sign in with their favorite social, company, or local identity accounts.

45. **Answer: B**

Explanation: Key Vault is a security service for managing keys in an encrypted form. It provides real-time usage logs of keys and protects them using Hardware Security Modules (HSM).

46. Answer: C

Explanation: Log Analytics in Azure is a comprehensive service designed for collecting, querying, and analyzing log and performance data from various sources across both on-premises and cloud environments. It supports real-time interactive querying using the Kusto Query Language (KQL) and provides powerful visualization capabilities through Azure Portal dashboards. With integrated alerting and monitoring features, Log Analytics enables proactive detection of issues and facilitates centralized management of system health and performance. It's a crucial tool for organizations seeking to optimize operations, ensure compliance, and enhance overall efficiency through centralized log management and analysis.

47. Answer: A

Explanation: Azure Monitor provides basic monitoring of Azure resources, helping you understand how your applications work and recognize challenges and tools that impact them proactively.

48. Answer: B

Explanation: IoT Hub is Azure's managed service for bi-directional communication between IoT devices and cloud solutions, supporting millions of devices with secure connectivity and integration with Azure services for real-time analytics and command execution.

49. Answer: A

Explanation: Azure Cognitive Search performs the full-text search using simple or lucent query syntax and enriches information for easy content recognition and discovery.

50. **Answer: C**

Explanation: Microsoft Defender for Cloud is a centralized network security management system that improves the security position of data centers and provides advanced threat safety through hybrid cloud workloads.

51. **Answer: B**

Explanation: Azure Blob Storage is a service designed to store massive amounts of unstructured data, such as text or binary data. It allows users to store and retrieve any amount of data at any time over HTTP or HTTPS, making it ideal for a variety of scenarios, including serving images or documents directly to a browser, storing files for distributed access, and streaming video and audio.

52. **Answer: C**

Explanation: Azure File Storage supports file shares up to 5TB in size, which makes it suitable for applications that require a shared file system. This service allows multiple virtual machines and cloud services to access and share the same files seamlessly, similar to a traditional on-premises file server. The file shares can be mounted concurrently by cloud or on-premises deployments of Windows, macOS, and Linux, offering a versatile solution for shared storage needs.

53. **Answer: C**

Explanation: Geo-Redundant Storage (GRS) in Azure replicates your data to a secondary region hundreds of miles away from the primary location. This ensures that your data is protected against regional outages, offering the highest level of durability and availability. If a primary region experiences a failure, GRS provides a backup in a different geographical area, enhancing data resilience and disaster recovery capabilities.

54. Answer: B

Explanation: Azure Queue Storage is a service designed for storing large numbers of messages that can be accessed from anywhere via authenticated calls using HTTP or HTTPS. It is typically used to create and manage asynchronous message queues, enabling reliable provisioning and communication between components of distributed applications. This ensures that messages are processed efficiently and in the order they were added, supporting scalable and decoupled architecture.

55. Answer: B

Explanation: Azure Table Storage is a NoSQL data storage service that uses a schema-less design, meaning it does not require a predefined structure for the stored data. This allows for flexible and dynamic data storage, as developers can easily adapt and add new attributes to their data without modifying existing schemas. It uses key/attribute pairs to store and retrieve data, making it efficient for managing structured, non-relational data at scale.

56. Answer: B

Explanation: Azure Data Lake Store is a scalable repository designed for big data analytics workloads. It is compatible with Hadoop Distributed File System (HDFS), which means it can work seamlessly with Hadoop-based services and applications. This compatibility allows for the efficient storage and processing of large amounts of structured and unstructured data, facilitating advanced analytics and data mining tasks.

57. Answer: C

Explanation: Azure Queue Storage allows messages to be up to 64 KB in size. This means that each message placed in a queue can contain up to 64 KB of data, making it suitable for storing and processing relatively small chunks of information. This capacity is ideal for scenarios where messages are used to communicate between different components of a distributed application, ensuring reliable and asynchronous message delivery.

58. Answer: C

Explanation: Azure HDInsight is an open-source, fully managed analytic service designed to process large amounts of data efficiently. It utilizes managed Hadoop clusters to provide a scalable and cost-effective platform for big data processing, analysis, and storage. HDInsight supports a variety of open-source frameworks, including Apache Hadoop, Spark, Hive, LLAP, Kafka, Storm, and HBase, allowing users to leverage familiar tools and frameworks to handle their big data needs in the cloud.

59. Answer: B

Explanation: Azure Cosmos DB is a globally distributed, multi-model database service designed to enable seamless scaling and high availability. It supports various data models, including document (SQL API), key-value (Table API), graph (Gremlin API), and column-family (Cassandra API), as well as MongoDB. Azure Cosmos DB's turnkey global distribution allows data to be replicated across multiple regions, providing low-latency access and high availability.

60. Answer: B

Explanation: Azure Redis Cache is a managed in-memory caching service provided by Microsoft Azure, built on the open-source Redis database. It accelerates application performance by storing data in memory, enabling fast read and write operations compared to traditional disk-based storage. Azure Redis Cache supports flexible scaling options seamless integration with Redis clients and libraries, and offers various data structures for sophisticated caching strategies. It's well-suited for applications needing high throughput, low latency data access, and efficient data sharing across distributed environments in the cloud.

61. Answer: B

Explanation: A resource in Azure is any manageable item, such as virtual machines, databases, or storage accounts, that can be deployed and managed through Azure Resource Manager. Each resource has its unique properties and settings and is organized within resource groups for logical management. Azure resources can be provisioned, monitored, and scaled through various Azure management interfaces like the portal, CLI, or PowerShell, facilitated by Azure Resource Manager for unified control over cloud infrastructure and applications.

62. Answer: C

Explanation: Resource Groups are used to deploy and manage resources in Azure. They act like containers where all resources of a solution or the resources that you want to manage together reside.

63. Answer: C

Explanation: When you delete a Resource Group in Azure, all the resources contained within it are also deleted simultaneously. This includes virtual machines, databases, storage accounts, and any other services provisioned under that Resource Group. Azure Resource Groups serve as logical containers for organizing and managing resources, facilitating easier deployment, monitoring, and cleanup. Deleting a Resource Group ensures that all associated resources and their data are removed, helping to streamline resource management and optimize costs within the Azure environment.

64. Answer: C

Explanation: Azure Resource Manager does not enforce billing boundaries; this is handled at the subscription level. ARM focuses on deploying, managing, and organizing resources.

65. Answer: B

Explanation: A Resource Provider supplies the resources for the Resource Manager by defining a set of REST operations for working with specific resources like Key Vaults, storage accounts, etc.

66. Answer: C

Explanation: Azure Resource Manager Templates are JSON files used to define and deploy Azure infrastructure. They include configurations for resources such as virtual machines, databases, and networks, along with parameters, variables, and outputs. JSON format is chosen for its readability, structure, and compatibility across platforms. Templates facilitate consistent and repeatable deployments, automate infrastructure management, and enable version control and collaboration. They play a crucial role in Infrastructure as Code (IaC) practices, ensuring reliable and scalable Azure deployments.

67. Answer: B

Explanation: Resource Locks in Azure are used to prevent accidental deletion or modification of resources. There are two types of locks: Delete Lock, which prevents deletion of a resource but allows modifications, and Read-Only Lock, which prevents any changes to the resource, including both read and write operations. These locks are essential for maintaining stability and compliance in Azure environments, ensuring critical resources remain secure from unintended actions. They can be managed and removed easily through Azure management interfaces like the portal, CLI, PowerShell, or Resource Manager templates.

68. Answer: C

Explanation: Tags allow you to improve the organization of your resources by associating custom details, such as cost center or billing department.

69. Answer: C

Explanation: An Azure subscription is essentially a billing account that grants you access to Azure services. It is the mechanism through which you are identified and authorized to use Azure resources.

70. **Answer: C**

Explanation: Multiple subscriptions can be created to separate billing for different environments like production and development to better manage and track costs.

71. **Answer: C**

Explanation: High Availability in cloud computing ensures that failed servers are quickly replaced with new ones, maintaining the availability of services.

72. **Answer: B**

Explanation: Fault tolerance is the design principle that ensures a system continues to operate smoothly even in the event of hardware or software failures. It involves incorporating redundancy and automated recovery mechanisms to quickly address and mitigate faults, thereby maintaining continuous availability and minimizing downtime.

73. **Answer: C**

Explanation: Disaster Recovery aims to restore business operations and IT systems to normalcy after a catastrophic event, such as a natural disaster, cyberattack, or major hardware failure. It involves strategies and processes for data backup, system recovery, and continuity planning to minimize the impact of such disruptions on business operations.

74. **Answer: B**

Explanation: Scalability in computing refers to the capability of a system to handle increasing workloads or to be easily expanded to accommodate growth. It involves the ability to dynamically allocate resources such as processing power, memory, storage, and network bandwidth in response to changing demand. Scalability ensures that applications and services can maintain performance and availability as workload fluctuates, either by adding more resources during peak times or scaling down during periods of lower demand. This flexibility is crucial for optimizing costs, improving performance, and providing a seamless user experience in cloud environments like Azure.

75. Answer: B

Explanation: Vertical scaling, or scaling up, increases the capacity of a single server by adding more CPU, memory, or storage resources. It's a straightforward approach to handle increased workload but has limits in scalability and hardware constraints.

76. Answer: C

Explanation: Software as a Service (SaaS) involves delivering applications over the internet as a service. Providers host and maintain the software, managing everything from infrastructure and security to updates and support. This allows users to access the software through a web browser without needing to install or manage it locally.

77. Answer: B

Explanation: Management of the cloud involves automating the deployment, scaling, and management of resources based on demand. This automation ensures that resources are provisioned and scaled up or down dynamically to meet application requirements efficiently and cost-effectively. By leveraging automation tools and techniques, organizations can achieve greater agility, reduce operational overhead, and optimize resource utilization in the cloud environment.

78. Answer: B

Explanation: Horizontal scaling, also known as scaling out, involves adding more servers or instances to a system to handle increasing load or to improve performance. This approach distributes the workload across multiple servers rather than increasing the capacity of a single server. Horizontal scaling is typically used in distributed systems and cloud environments where adding more instances allows applications to handle higher traffic volumes, improve fault tolerance, and achieve better performance scalability. It contrasts with vertical scaling (scaling up), which involves increasing the capacity of individual servers or resources.

79. Answer: B

Explanation: Platform as a Service (PaaS) is designed to support the complete application life cycle, including building, testing, deploying, managing, and updating applications.

80. Answer: B

Explanation: Cloud governance involves a set of practices to ensure that users operate in the cloud efficiently and in ways that they want, allowing for monitoring and correction of operations as needed.

81. Answer: B

Explanation: Azure Management Groups provide a level of scope above subscriptions to help keep track of access, regulations, and compliance for all Azure subscriptions.

82. Answer: D

Explanation: Azure Logic Apps can be triggered by various events, including HTTP requests, time-based schedules, and events from services like storage accounts. However, Azure Blob versioning is not a trigger type for Logic Apps. Triggers generally involve operations that start workflows based on specific events or schedules.

83. Answer: A

Explanation: Azure App Service is a PaaS that provides a managed platform for hosting web applications, mobile app back-ends, RESTful APIs, and automated business processes.

84. Answer: C

Explanation: In Azure, a single directory acts like a filing cabinet for the organization. It can hold a massive amount of information, up to 10,000 management groups, which help categorize and manage your cloud resources. This allows for efficient organization even with complex setups.

85. Answer: C

Explanation: Azure Batch is a managed service for batch processing jobs and running large-scale parallel and High-Performance Computing (HPC) Applications.

86. Answer: C

Explanation: Azure CDN provides high bandwidth content delivery by caching content on edge servers at Point of Presence (PoP) locations near end-users to reduce latency.

87. Answer: C

Explanation: You can create a hierarchical structure with up to six layers of management groups beneath the root management group. However, this doesn't include the root management group itself, nor does it include the subscription level, which is the final level in the hierarchy.

88. Answer: C

Explanation: Azure Functions are billed based on the number of executions, the execution time, and the resources consumed during the execution. This allows for a pay-as-you-go model where you only pay for the actual usage of your functions, making it cost-effective for varying workloads.

89. Answer: B

Explanation: Azure ExpressRoute provides dedicated private connections between Azure data centers and on-premises locations or Azure data centers. It offers higher bandwidth, lower latency, and more reliability compared to public internet connections.

90. Answer: B

Explanation: Azure Management Groups can be used to centralize user access management across multiple subscriptions, simplifying access control by leveraging Azure Role-Based Access Control (Azure RBAC).

91. Answer: C

Explanation: An Azure region is defined as a geographical area on the planet that contains at least one, but potentially multiple, data centers that are networked together with a low-latency network. This organization allows for better scalability, redundancy, and data residency for services.

92. Answer: C

Explanation: Azure's extensive network of global regions allows users to deploy their applications in locations closer to where their users are, providing lower latency and a better user experience while also offering improved scalability and redundancy.

93. Answer: C

Explanation: Azure geography refers to a discrete market that is typically made up of two or more regions, which are defined by geopolitical boundaries or country borders. This helps in preserving data residency and compliance within those geographical limits.

94. Answer: B

Explanation: Azure geographies are important because they allow customers to meet specific data residency and compliance needs by keeping their data and applications close. They ensure that data residency, sovereignty, compliance, and resiliency requirements are respected within the geographical boundaries.

95. Answer: C

Explanation: Data residency refers to the physical or geographic location where an organization's data is stored. This concept is crucial for complying with legal or regulatory requirements that are imposed on data based on the country or region in which it resides.

96. Answer: B

Explanation: Azure geographies are designed to be fault-tolerant and can withstand complete region failure through their connection to dedicated high-capacity networking infrastructure. This ensures continuous service and compliance with data residency requirements even in the face of regional outages.

97. Answer: C

Explanation: Azure divides the world into geographies that include the Americas, Europe, Asia Pacific, Middle East, and Africa. Each region within these geographies has specific service availability, compliance, and data residency/sovereignty rules applied to it.

98. Answer: C

Explanation: Organizing data centers into regions allows Azure to intelligently assign and control resources within each region, ensuring that workloads are appropriately balanced. This structure also supports better scalability and redundancy for the services offered.

99. Answer: D

Explanation: Azure regions are geographical areas that can contain multiple data centers networked together with a low-latency network. This interconnected setup helps provide better service and redundancy for deployed applications.

100. Answer: D

Explanation: Although availability zones are a part of Azure's infrastructure, providing high availability within regions, they are not explicitly described in the provided context. The context focuses on regions and geographies without detailing availability zones.

101. Answer: C

Explanation: Azure Resource Manager allows you to deploy, update, or delete all the resources for your solution in a single, coordinated operation, making it easier to manage the infrastructure as a cohesive unit.

102. Answer: B

Explanation: Azure Resource Manager encourages the use of declarative templates for deployment and configuration, eliminating the need for imperative commands for setting up resources.

103. Answer: B

Explanation: Azure Resource Manager templates use declarative syntax, allowing you to state the desired resources and properties without writing sequences of programming commands.

104. **Answer: B**

Explanation: A resource in Azure refers to an individual component or service that you can manage and utilize within Azure, such as virtual machines, storage accounts, databases, and more.

105. **Answer: C**

Explanation: A resource group in Azure is a logical container that holds related resources like virtual machines, databases, and storage accounts. It helps in organizing and managing these resources as a single entity for tasks like deployment, monitoring, and access control. Resource groups also act as a scope for applying policies, tags, and role-based access controls across multiple resources at once.

106. **Answer: D**

Explanation: All the listed Azure tools—Azure PowerShell, Azure CLI, and the Azure portal—can interact with the Azure Resource Manager (ARM) API. Each tool provides a different interface for managing and interacting with Azure resources through ARM.

107. **Answer: B**

Explanation: A resource provider in Azure Resource Manager is responsible for implementing operations related to specific types of resources, such as creating, updating, and managing those resources. It essentially provides the necessary functionality and APIs for interacting with and managing the resources it handles.

108. **Answers: C**

Explanation: In Azure Resource Manager, resource type names are structured as `{resource-provider}/{resource-type}`. This format helps uniquely identify each type of resource within Azure. The `resource-provider` specifies the service or technology offering the resource. At the same time, `resource-type` identifies the specific type of resource, such as `Microsoft.Compute/virtual machines` for virtual machines or `Microsoft.Storage/storage accounts` for storage accounts. This naming convention ensures clarity and consistency when managing and referencing resources across Azure deployments.

109. Answer: C

Explanation: Tags in Azure Resource Manager allow you to categorize and organize resources based on various criteria, such as department, project, or environment. This helps in tracking and analyzing costs more effectively, as you can filter and group resources by tags to better understand and manage billing and expenses.

110. Answer: C

Explanation: Azure Resource Manager (ARM) templates use JSON to define and deploy infrastructure and configuration in a declarative manner. This approach allows you to specify the desired state of resources, which can be reused and deployed across different environments with minimal manual intervention.

111. Answer: B

Explanation: In Azure, deployments are incremental, meaning adding new resources to a resource group will not impact the existing resources. This approach allows for seamless updates and expansions without disrupting current operations. Existing resources remain intact and operational during the deployment of additional resources.

112. Answer: C

Explanation: Resource groups in Azure can include resources located in different regions. This flexibility allows for centralized management and organization of resources, regardless of their geographic location. It enables efficient handling and deployment of multi-region solutions.

113. Answer: C

Explanation: If a resource requires a different deployment cycle, it should be placed in a separate resource group. This separation allows for independent management, updates, and scaling of resources without affecting others. It ensures better control and flexibility over deployment processes.

114. Answer: C

Explanation: The location of the resource group specifies where the metadata about the resources is stored. This means that the resource group's region determines where information about its resources is maintained, ensuring optimal performance and compliance.

115. Answer: B

Explanation: Resource Manager locks prevent the accidental deletion or modification of resources by putting a structure in place. This adds an extra layer of protection by restricting certain operations on critical resources, ensuring their stability and continuity.

116. Answer: B

Explanation: Read-only locks prevent any changes to the resource by restricting all write operations. This ensures that the resource's configuration remains unchanged while still allowing read operations.

117. Answer: C

Explanation: During the move operation, both the source group and the target group are locked, which blocks all write and delete operations. This ensures the integrity of the resources during the transition process, preventing any changes that could disrupt the move.

118. **Answer: C**

Explanation: Resources can interact with each other even if they are in different resource groups. This allows for flexibility in organizing and managing resources while maintaining connectivity and interaction capabilities across different groups.

119. **Answer: B**

Explanation: Resource groups cannot be renamed according to the given rules. If you need a resource group with a different name, you must create a new one and move the resources to it.

120. **Answer: C**

Explanation: Delete locks are a feature in Azure that prevents the accidental deletion of resources. When applied, they ensure that resources cannot be deleted until the lock is removed. This helps safeguard critical resources from being unintentionally removed.

121. **Answer: B**

Explanation: Azure Cloud Shell is an interactive, browser-based command-line interface provided by Azure. It allows users to manage Azure resources directly from the browser without needing to install or configure any local tools. Cloud Shell comes pre-configured with popular Azure tools and supports both PowerShell and Bash environments. It also provides persistent cloud storage for saving files between sessions, making it convenient for managing Azure resources from anywhere with internet access.

122. Answer: B

Explanation: Azure Cloud Shell is indeed managed by Microsoft, ensuring users have access to the latest versions of Azure CLI and PowerShell modules without needing to manage updates locally. This centralized management approach ensures that users can leverage the newest features and improvements seamlessly, enhancing the overall reliability and efficiency of managing Azure resources from the browser-based command-line interface.

123. Answer: C

Explanation: Azure Cloud Shell indeed offers cloud storage associated with the user's Azure subscription. This feature allows users to persist files such as scripts, SSH keys, configurations, and other data between different Cloud Shell sessions. This capability ensures continuity and convenience by making essential files accessible across sessions and devices, enhancing the overall usability of Azure Cloud Shell for managing and automating Azure resources.

124. Answer: A

Explanation: Azure Cloud Shell provides a command-line interface (CLI) for managing Azure resources directly from a web browser or the Azure mobile app. It includes pre-installed tools like Azure CLI and Azure PowerShell, enabling users to create, configure, and manage various Azure services such as virtual machines (VMs), storage accounts, networking components, and more. This capability makes it convenient for users to perform administrative tasks and automation tasks without needing to install additional software locally, leveraging the flexibility and accessibility of the cloud-based command-line environment.

125. Answer: C

Explanation: Azure Cloud Shell operates within an infrastructure that ensures data is encrypted at rest by default. This means all data stored within Cloud Shell, including files, scripts, and configurations, is automatically encrypted to enhance security. This encryption helps protect sensitive information from unauthorized access or breaches, ensuring compliance with industry standards and regulatory requirements for data security in cloud environments.

126. Answer: B

Explanation: Cloud Shell sessions automatically terminate after 20 minutes of inactivity to optimize resource usage and maintain security. This ensures that resources allocated to idle sessions are released promptly, contributing to the efficient management of Azure's cloud infrastructure. Users are notified before session termination to prevent data loss and allow them to save work.

127. Answer: C

Explanation: In Azure Cloud Shell, users can choose between PowerShell and Bash command-line interfaces based on their preference and familiarity, providing flexibility in managing Azure resources and performing tasks efficiently.

128. Answer: A

Explanation: You can access Azure Cloud Shell directly from code snippets embedded within Microsoft Learn modules, enabling hands-on learning and direct application of Azure commands without needing to switch between environments.

129. Answer: C

Explanation: Azure Cloud Shell can be accessed via a direct link, through the Azure portal, or from code snippets in Microsoft Learn, but not from a physical Azure store.

130. Answer: C

Explanation: Azure Cloud Shell is a web-based tool, so if your session terminates, you can simply start a new session from the Azure portal or via the direct link. There's no need to contact support, restart your computer, or reinstall the Azure CLI.

131. Answer: D

Explanation: Azure Cloud Shell comes preconfigured with tools like Ansible, Terraform, and Chef. However, Apache Tomcat is not listed among the preconfigured tools in Azure Cloud Shell.

132. Answer: C

Explanation: Azure Cloud Shell sessions automatically disconnect after 20 minutes of inactivity to help manage resources and ensure security. This is a known limitation, though Cloud Shell offers many features and capabilities for managing Azure resources.

133. Answer: A

Explanation: Azure Cloud Shell provides both the Azure CLI and the Azure classic CLI, enabling users to manage and interact with Azure resources through either command-line interface. This versatility allows for flexible and efficient resource management directly from the cloud.

134. Answer: B

Explanation: Azure Cloud Shell does not support opening multiple sessions at the same time and is not suitable for concurrent work across multiple subscriptions or tenants.

135. Answer: C

Explanation: Azure Cloud Shell offers several text editors, including Vim, Nano, and Emacs, allowing users to edit files directly within the command-line environment according to their preferences.

136. Answer: B

Explanation: Azure Cloud Shell storage is limited to a single region, and users might need to back up and synchronize content since only one region can have the storage allocated.

137. Answer: B

Explanation: Azure Cloud Shell comes with utility tools like Docker, Kubectl, and Helm pre-installed, enabling seamless management of containerized applications and Kubernetes clusters directly from the command-line interface.

138. Answer: C

Explanation: Azure Cloud Shell does not provide admin permissions such as sudo access within the environment, ensuring that users operate with restricted privileges to maintain security and stability.

139. Answer: C

Explanation: Azure Cloud Shell includes container orchestration tools like DC/OS CLI and Kubernetes (Kubectl), providing users with the capability to manage and deploy containerized applications directly from the command-line interface.

140. Answer: B

Explanation: Azure Cloud Shell is suitable for persisting files between sessions for later use, among other tasks like interacting with Azure resources from any browser-based device.

141. Answer: B

Explanation: The `ls` command in Bash is used to display the contents of the current working directory, showing files and directories. It helps users quickly see what is present in their current location within the filesystem.

142. Answer: C

Explanation: In Unix-like operating systems, the -a flag (or --all) with the ls command shows all files and directories, including those that are hidden (those starting with a dot .).

143. Answer: C

Explanation: You can combine flags by placing them together after a single hyphen. For example, -a and -l can be combined as -al to list all files including hidden ones with detailed information.

144. Answer: B

Explanation: The man command stands for "manual" and is used in Unix-like operating systems to access the system's documentation for various commands, utilities, and functions. When you run man mkdir, it opens the manual page for the mkdir command, which provides detailed information about its usage, options, and syntax.

145. Answer: B

Explanation: The `--help` option, when used with a command, displays a brief description of the command's syntax and available options. It serves as a quick reference guide for users to understand how to use the command and what parameters it accepts.

146. Answer: B

Explanation: PowerShell is a shell developed by Microsoft for Windows, although it has been made available on Linux and macOS as well. The commonly used shells in Linux are Bash (Bourne Again Shell), csh (C Shell), and zsh (Z Shell).

147. Answer: B

Explanation: Bash is a Unix shell and command language that is an enhanced version of the original Bourne Shell (sh). It includes features from the Bourne Shell as well as additional capabilities.

148. Answer: C

Explanation: Unix design philosophy emphasizes creating simple, single-purpose programs that can be combined to perform complex tasks. These programs should work independently and communicate through text streams, ensuring interoperability and flexibility. While graphical interfaces are not a core principle of Unix philosophy, using text streams and maintaining program independence are central to the Unix approach.

149. Answer: A

Explanation: The command `ls /etc/` displays the contents of the `/etc` directory in a Unix-like operating system. This includes configuration files and subdirectories. It provides an overview of all files and directories within `/etc.`.

150. Answer: B

Explanation: The man command is used to access the manual pages that provide detailed documentation for various commands and utilities in Unix-like operating systems. This includes information about usage, options, and syntax for commands.

151. Answer: B

Explanation: The * wildcard is used in pattern matching to match any number of characters, including none. It is commonly used in commands and scripts to represent multiple files or directories that fit a certain pattern.

152. Answer: C

Explanation: The command `ls *.png` in Unix-like systems lists all files in the current directory that have names ending with the `.png` extension. It matches and displays filenames such as `image1.png`, `logo.png`, and `photo.png`, but excludes files with different extensions or no extensions. This wildcard pattern (`*.png`) is useful for filtering and viewing specific types of files based on their file extensions.

153. Answer: A

Explanation: The command `ls *.jp*g` in Unix-like systems lists all files in the current directory that have names ending with `.jpg` or `.jpeg`. The asterisk (`*`) wildcard matches any sequence of characters, including none, before the characters `jp` and any characters after it, followed by `g`. This allows the command to list files such as `image1.jpg`, `photo.jpeg`, and `pic.jpg`, effectively covering both common variations of the JPEG image file extension.

154. Answer: B

Explanation: The ? wildcard matches exactly one character in pattern matching. It is used when you need to match a single character in a filename or string.

155. Answer: C

Explanation: The command `ls [0-9]*` in Unix-like systems lists all files in the current directory whose names start with a digit (0-9). The square brackets (`[0-9]`) denote a character class that matches any single digit from 0 to 9. The asterisk (`*`) wildcard matches any sequence of characters following the digit. Therefore, this command will list files such as `1file`, `2.txt`, `3image.jpg`, and so on, but not files whose names start with letters or other characters.

156. Answer: A

Explanation: The command `ls *.[jp]*` in Unix-like systems is used to list files in the current directory that have filenames containing a period (`.`) followed by either a lowercase 'j' or 'p'. It leverages wildcards to match specific patterns in filenames, helping users quickly identify and list files with extensions like `.jpg`, `.jpeg`, or any other where the filename contains 'j' or 'p'. This flexibility in file matching is essential for managing and organizing files efficiently from the command line.

157. Answer: A

Explanation: The asterisk (*) in [A-Z]* acts as a wildcard, matching zero or more uppercase letters (A-Z). So, ls [A-Z]* instructs the ls command to list all filenames that start with an uppercase letter, followed by any number of characters (including zero).

158. Answer: B

Explanation: This command lists all files where the last character in the filename is a digit. The * wildcard matches any sequence of characters, and [0-9] ensures that the filename ends with a digit.

159. Answer: C

Explanation: This command matches files where the name includes a period followed by either 'j', 'p', 'J', or 'P'. The pattern *.[jpJP]* ensures that the file name has any sequence of characters before and after the period and matches the specified letters.

160. Answer: B

Explanation: The backslash (\) is used to escape the wildcard character, so it is treated as a literal asterisk rather than a wildcard. This ensures that the search looks for files with an actual asterisk in their names.

161. Answer: D

Explanation: Azure Kubernetes Service (AKS) provides managed Kubernetes, integrated CI/CD, and automated upgrades and patching, allowing easy deployment and management of containerized applications. However, AKS does not include built-in SQL database support as a feature. While you can deploy SQL databases in AKS, it is not an inherent feature of the service.

162. Answer: C

Explanation: In Unix-like operating systems, files and directories that start with a dot (.) are considered hidden. By default, the ls command does not display these hidden files. The -a flag, which stands for "all," modifies the ls command to include these hidden files in the listing.

163. Answer: A

Explanation: The -l flag stands for "long format" and provides detailed information about each file or directory, including permissions, number of links, owner, group, size, and the last modification date and time. This format offers a comprehensive view of file attributes and metadata.

164. Answer: C

Explanation: The `cat` command in Linux is used to concatenate and display the contents of a file on the terminal. It's commonly used to view text files, displaying their entire contents sequentially.

165. Answer: B

Explanation: The cat command displays the content of the specified file, in this case, /etc/os-release, which typically contains information about the operating system.

166. Answer: D

Explanation: The long format output of `ls -l` includes permissions, owner, group, size, modification date, and the file or directory name, but not the contents of the file.

167. Answer: C

Explanation: The `/etc` directory in Unix-like operating systems such as Linux contains system-configuration files. These files are essential for the system's operation and configuration of various applications and services installed on the system.

168. Answer: B

Explanation: In Linux, files and directories starting with a period (.) are considered hidden. They do not appear in the default output of commands like ls unless the -a flag is used. This convention helps keep configuration and system files from cluttering the view of regular files.

169. Answer: B

Explanation: The `-a` flag lists all files, including hidden ones, and the `-l` flag lists them in long format. Combined, `ls -al` shows detailed information for all files, including hidden ones.

170. Answer: D

Explanation: Azure offers several types of storage accounts, including General-purpose v2 (which supports blobs, files, queues, and tables), Blob Storage (optimized for storing unstructured data), and Queue Storage (for reliable messaging between applications). However, SQL Storage is not a type of Azure Storage account. Instead, Azure provides SQL Database as a managed relational database service.

171. Answer: C

Explanation: In Unix-like systems, the `>>` operator is used to redirect the output of a command and append it to a file. This prevents overwriting the existing content of the file and adds new content at the end.

172. Answer: C

Explanation: The command sort < data.txt > sorted_data.txt reads the contents of data.txt, sorts them, and then redirects the sorted output to a new file named sorted_data.txt. This effectively sorts the data from data.txt and saves the sorted results in sorted_data.txt.

173. Answer: A

Explanation: The `<` operator in Unix-like systems is indeed used to redirect input from a file instead of from the keyboard. This allows commands to read input directly from a specified file, which can be useful for automating tasks or processing data stored in files without manual input.

174. Answer: B

Explanation: This command first lists all currently running processes with ps -ef, then pipes (|) the output to grep daemon., which filters and displays only the lines that contain the string "daemon.".

175. Answer: D

Explanation: The `>>` operator in Unix-like systems is used to append output to a file. If the file (`listing.txt` in this case) already exists, using `>>` will append the output to the end of the file without overwriting its existing content. This is particularly useful for logging or accumulating data over multiple command executions.

176. Answer: B

Explanation: The `head` command in Unix-like systems is used to display the first few lines of a file or input stream. By default, it shows the first 10 lines, but this can be adjusted using the `-n` option followed by a number to specify the desired number of lines. For example, `ps -ef | head` would display the first 10 lines of the output from the `ps -ef` command, showing details of running processes on the system.

177. Answer: D

Explanation: The | operator, known as a pipe, takes the output of one command and uses it as the input for the next command. This allows for the chaining of commands and the creation of complex command sequences.

178. Answer: C

Explanation: The command cat file.txt | fmt | pr | lpr involves multiple stages of text processing, culminating in sending the output to the printer. cat reads the contents of file.txt, which is then formatted into tidy paragraphs by fmt. The pr command paginates the formatted text, adding necessary headers, footers, and page breaks to prepare it for printing. Finally, lpr (line printer) sends this paginated output to the printer, effectively printing the processed text. Therefore, lpr is used to send the paginated output to the printer, completing the chain of command.

179. Answer: A

Explanation: The `more` command in Unix-like systems is used to view the contents of a file one screen at a time. It pauses after each screenful of information, allowing you to scroll through the output. Pressing the spacebar moves to the next page, and pressing `q` quits the display. It's useful for viewing large files or long command outputs without overwhelming the terminal window.

180. Answer: A

Explanation: The correct syntax to redirect both input and output in Unix-like systems is true: `cmd < input > output`. This command redirects the standard input of `cmd` from the `input` file and directs the standard output to the `output` file. It's commonly used for automation and scripting tasks where command output needs to be saved to a file or input needs to be provided from a file rather than interactively.

181. Answer: A

Explanation: PowerShell consists of a command-line shell, which lacks a graphical interface, and a scripting language used for automating administrative tasks and other kinds of tasks.

182. Answer: B

Explanation: Using a console is ideal for task automation, especially in continuous-integration pipelines, because you can run batches of commands.

183. Answer: C

Explanation: Storing commands and scripts in a text file allows the use of source-control systems, making the commands repeatable and auditable.

184. Answer: C

Explanation: Unlike traditional command-line shells that work primarily with text, PowerShell operates with objects. This allows for more complex and structured manipulation of data, enabling users to handle output as objects with properties and methods, which can be further processed and piped through the system.

185. Answer: C

Explanation: Cmdlets are built-in commands in PowerShell that are based on a common runtime, providing consistency in parameter parsing and pipeline behavior.

186. Answer: B

Explanation: Aliases in PowerShell provide shorthand names for cmdlets or commands, making it easier to use commands with shorter or more familiar names.

187. Answer: C

Explanation: PowerShell uses a pipeline to run many commands sequentially, where the output of one command serves as the input for the next.

188. Answer: B

Explanation: PowerShell itself is built on .NET Core, which is open-source and cross-platform. PowerShell Core includes a set of core cmdlets that are compatible with .NET Core, allowing for the management and automation of tasks across different operating systems like Windows, macOS, and various Linux distributions. This flexibility and openness make PowerShell Core a versatile tool for managing environments that span multiple platforms.

189. Answer: C

Explanation: PowerShell allows for extensibility through the creation of custom cmdlets, scripts, and functions, enabling users to add new functionality and automate tasks according to their needs.

190. Answer: D

Explanation: PowerShell commands encompass a range of types, including native executables, cmdlets, functions, scripts, and aliases, providing flexibility in how tasks can be performed and automated.

191. Answer: A

Explanation: A cmdlet is a lightweight command used in the PowerShell environment, developed in .NET or .NET Core, and can be invoked within PowerShell.

192. Answer: B

Explanation: The Get-Command cmdlet retrieves a list of all cmdlets, functions, workflows, aliases, and scripts that are available in your PowerShell session.

193. Answer: C

Explanation: The -Noun flag targets the part of the command name that's related to the noun. The example Get-Command -Noun alias* searches for all cmdlets whose noun part starts with "alias".

194. Answer: A

Explanation: The Get-Verb cmdlet provides a list of the verbs that can be used in cmdlet names, helping to understand the standard actions that cmdlets perform.

195. Answer: B

Explanation: The Get-Help cmdlet displays detailed information about cmdlets, functions, workflows, aliases, and scripts, including their syntax, parameters, and usage examples.

196. Answer: C

Explanation: The Get-Member cmdlet allows you to drill down into the response object returned by a command to learn more about its properties and methods.

197. Answer: B

Explanation: The -Verb flag targets the part of the command name that's related to the verb. For example, Get-Command -Verb Add will list all cmdlets that have "Add" as their verb.

198. Answer: C

Explanation: Visual Studio Code with the PowerShell extension is recommended for authoring and running PowerShell scripts as it offers features like snippets, code completion, and syntax highlighting.

199. Answer: A

Explanation: The help command can be used as an alias for Get-Help, and piping it to more (help <cmdlet> | more) paginates the response for a better reading experience.

200. Answer: B

Explanation: The -Verb and -Noun flags are used with the Get-Command cmdlet to filter the list of commands to quickly locate the specific command you need based on its verb or noun.

201. Answer: A

Explanation: Resource Manager templates automate the deployment process, allowing for faster and more consistent deployments without manual intervention.

202. Answer: C

Explanation: Resource Manager templates in Azure are written in JSON, allowing for a structured and consistent definition of resources. JSON's readability and flexibility enable declarative configuration of Azure resources, making deployments repeatable and manageable. These templates support parameters for customization, variables for simplification, and outputs for returning resource information. This approach ensures predictable and automated deployment of infrastructure.

203. Answer: B

Explanation: The $schema element specifies the URL to the JSON schema file that describes the structure and validation rules for the template, ensuring it adheres to the expected format and schema for resource definitions.

204. Answer: B

Explanation: Resource Manager templates ensure that resources are deployed in the correct order by mapping out each resource and its dependent resources.

205. Answer: C

Explanation: The "parameters" section allows you to define input values that can be customized at deployment time, enabling flexibility and reusability of the template across different environments or scenarios.

206. Answer: D

Explanation: The "resources" element in a Resource Manager template is essential for specifying the Azure resources to be deployed. It outlines the types and configurations of resources such as virtual machines, storage accounts, and networks. This section ensures that the template clearly defines what needs to be created or managed. It is a critical part of the template, enabling the actual deployment of resources in Azure.

207. Answer: B

Explanation: Resource Manager templates support linking to other templates, enabling modular design and reuse of common configurations. This approach allows you to build complex deployments by combining smaller, reusable templates.

208. Answer: C

Explanation: The "outputs" section specifies values that should be returned after the deployment is completed, such as resource IDs or other information useful for further processing or integration.

209. Answer: C

Explanation: Using revision control systems like GIT allows you to track changes, manage different versions, and document the evolution of your deployment templates. This practice enhances collaboration, auditing, and rollback capabilities.

210. Answer: C

Explanation: Template parameters allow for customization, enabling the same template to be used for different environments, such as staging and production.

211. Answer: B

Explanation: The maximum number of parameters allowed in an ARM template is indeed **256**. This limit helps ensure manageable and efficient template configuration.

212. Answer: A

Explanation: The type property of a parameter in an ARM template specifies the kind of value it can hold, such as string, int, or boolean. This property ensures that the input values adhere to the expected format and type, facilitating proper template functioning and validation.

213. Answer: C

Explanation: The "allowed values" property specifies a set of predefined values that the parameter can accept, ensuring that only valid options are used in the deployment.

214. Answer: D

Explanation: Bicep provides simpler syntax, modules for easier management and automatic dependency management, but it does not increase the parameter limit beyond 256.

215. Answer: B

Explanation: Bicep automatically manages and detects dependencies between resources based on their references in the code. This simplifies resource deployment by ensuring that resources are created in the correct order without requiring explicit dependency declarations.

216. Answer: C

Explanation: Transpilation is the process of converting source code written in one language into another language, which Bicep does to convert its syntax into JSON.

217. Answer: B

Explanation: The Bicep extension for Visual Studio Code enhances the development experience by offering features like IntelliSense and validation for Azure resource types and API definitions, making it easier to write and manage Bicep templates.

218. Answer: C

Explanation: The securestring parameter type ensures that sensitive information is handled securely, providing additional protection by masking or encrypting the data.

219. Answer: C

Explanation: The defaultValue property allows you to set a predefined value for a parameter that will be used if the user does not provide a different value during deployment.

220. Answer: C

Explanation: String interpolation in Bicep simplifies combining values for names and other items, making the syntax easier to read and write compared to concatenation in JSON.

221. Answer: A

Explanation: Azure Blob Storage is designed for storing large amounts of unstructured data like documents and media files. It offers high availability, durability, and scalability, making it suitable for a wide range of storage needs, including serving static assets for web applications and storing backups. Azure Blob Storage supports different access tiers to optimize costs based on access patterns and retention requirements.

222. **Answer:** B

Explanation: Azure Automation allows you to automate the deployment and management of Azure resources, including virtual machines (VMs). By using runbooks and workflows, Azure Automation helps streamline repetitive tasks such as VM provisioning, configuration management, and scaling operations. This automation reduces manual effort, improves consistency, and enhances operational efficiency across your Azure environment.

223. **Answer:** B

Explanation: Azure ExpressRoute provides a dedicated private connection between an on-premises network and Azure data centers or Microsoft cloud services. It offers predictable performance, lower latency, and enhanced security compared to connections over the public internet. ExpressRoute is ideal for scenarios where data privacy, regulatory compliance, and reliable connectivity are critical requirements.

224. **Answer:** A

Explanation: Azure Monitor is a comprehensive monitoring service that provides insights into the performance and health of Azure resources. It collects and analyzes telemetry data from applications and infrastructure, offering visibility into metrics, logs, and diagnostics. Azure Monitor helps you detect issues proactively, troubleshoot problems, and optimize performance by leveraging customizable alerts, dashboards, and integration with other Azure services.

225. **Answer:** B

Explanation: Azure Backup is a cloud-based service that provides backup and restore capabilities for Azure VMs, Azure Files, SQL databases, and more. It helps protect your data against accidental deletion, corruption, and ransomware attacks by creating recovery points and storing them securely in Azure. Azure Backup simplifies data protection management with centralized policy-based backups and flexible retention policies tailored to your business needs.

226. **Answer:** C

Explanation: Azure Key Vault is a secure management service that allows you to safeguard cryptographic keys, secrets, and certificates used by cloud applications and services. It provides centralized storage and management of sensitive information, eliminating the need to store keys and secrets within your application code. Azure Key Vault integrates with Entra ID for authentication and access control, ensuring that only authorized applications and users can access sensitive data.

227. **Answer:** B

Explanation: Azure DNS is a hosting service for domain name system (DNS) domains that provides name resolution using Microsoft Azure infrastructure. It enables you to manage DNS records for your domain names directly within Azure, simplifying domain management and reducing latency by leveraging Azure's global network of DNS servers. Azure DNS supports features such as custom domain names, DNS zone delegation, and integration with Azure services for automatic DNS record updates.

228. **Answer:** B

Explanation: The Contributor role in Azure allows users to manage all aspects of Azure resources except access to billing information. It grants permissions to create and manage all types of Azure resources, including virtual machines, databases, and storage accounts, without granting administrative privileges that could affect billing or access control settings.

229. Answer: C

Explanation: Azure Virtual Machine Scale Sets allow you to automatically scale the number of VM instances based on demand or a defined schedule. They provide elasticity for applications by automatically adding or removing VM instances in response to changing workload requirements. Virtual Machine Scale Sets simplify management by enabling you to define scaling policies and configure automatic scaling without manual intervention.

230. Answer: A

Explanation: Azure Storage Service Encryption (SSE) automatically encrypts data at rest in Azure Blob Storage using Microsoft-managed keys. SSE helps protect your data against unauthorized access by encrypting it before storing it on disk, ensuring that sensitive information remains secure even if physical disks are compromised or stolen. SSE integrates seamlessly with Azure Blob Storage, providing transparent encryption with minimal impact on performance and management overhead.

231. Answer: B

Explanation: Azure App Service is a fully managed platform-as-a-service (PaaS) offering that allows you to build, deploy, and scale web applications and APIs without managing the underlying infrastructure. It supports multiple programming languages, frameworks, and development tools, enabling rapid development and deployment cycles. Azure App Service includes built-in features such as automatic scaling, continuous deployment, and integration with Azure DevOps for seamless application lifecycle management.

232. Answer: C

Explanation: Azure Load Balancer distributes incoming network traffic across multiple VMs or instances to ensure high availability, scalability, and reliability of applications and services. It operates at the transport layer

(Layer 4) of the OSI model, allowing you to load balance traffic based on IP address and port. Azure Load Balancer supports both internal and external load balancing scenarios, helping you achieve optimal performance and fault tolerance for your applications.

233. **Answer:** D

Explanation: Azure Policy allows you to enforce organizational standards and compliance requirements by defining and applying rules (policies) to your Azure resources. One common use case for Azure Policy is enforcing resource tagging requirements, which helps ensure consistent metadata management and cost allocation across your Azure environment. By applying policies, you can enforce naming conventions, tag usage, and other governance standards to maintain visibility, control, and compliance.

234. **Answer:** B

Explanation: Azure Log Analytics is a service that collects and analyzes telemetry data from Azure resources, applications, and infrastructure. It provides advanced analytics, insights, and visualizations into the performance, health, and operational status of your Azure environment. Azure Log Analytics helps you identify trends, diagnose issues, and troubleshoot problems by correlating data from various sources and presenting actionable insights through customizable dashboards and reports.

235. **Answer:** B

Explanation: Azure Site Recovery is a disaster recovery service that helps protect and recover on-premises and Azure-based applications and workloads. It orchestrates replication, failover, and failback processes to ensure business continuity in case of disruptions, such as hardware failures, datacenter outages, or natural disasters. Azure Site Recovery provides automated recovery plans, non-disruptive testing, and integration with Azure Virtual Machines and VMware environments, simplifying disaster recovery management and minimizing downtime.

236. **Answer:** C

Explanation: Microsoft Defender for Cloud is a unified security management service that helps you prevent, detect, and respond to security threats across your Azure environment. It provides advanced threat protection for workloads, virtual machines, containers, and Azure services by continuously monitoring for security vulnerabilities, misconfigurations, and suspicious activities. Microsoft Defender for Cloud offers security recommendations, threat intelligence, and automated remediation to strengthen security posture and compliance with regulatory requirements.

237. **Answer:** A

Explanation: Azure ExpressRoute enhances connectivity to Azure by establishing dedicated private connections that bypass the public internet. It provides predictable performance, lower latency, and improved reliability compared to connections over the internet, making it suitable for scenarios requiring data privacy, compliance, and reliable access to Azure services. Azure ExpressRoute supports hybrid cloud deployments by enabling seamless integration between on-premises networks and Azure virtual networks, ensuring consistent connectivity and data transfer efficiency.

238. **Answer:** C

Explanation: Azure Archive Blob Storage offers the lowest storage costs but has higher data retrieval costs compared to the Hot and Cool tiers, making it suitable for long-term data storage with infrequent access.

239. **Answer:** B

Explanation: Azure Availability Sets ensure high availability and fault tolerance by distributing VM instances across multiple physical servers within a datacenter to minimize downtime during hardware failures or planned maintenance.

240. **Answer:** A

Explanation: Azure Virtual Network peering enables you to connect virtual networks (VNets) within the same Azure region, allowing resources in peered VNets to communicate securely without the need for gateways.

241. **Answer:** C

Explanation: Azure Monitor allows you to configure alerts to notify you when specific conditions are met based on metrics, events, and logs collected from Azure resources, helping you proactively monitor and manage your Azure environment.

242. **Answer:** C

Explanation: Azure Site Recovery provides disaster recovery as a service (DRaaS) for on-premises and Azure virtual machines, enabling replication, failover, and failback to ensure business continuity during disruptions.

243. **Answer:** C

Explanation: Azure Key Vault uses role-based access control (RBAC) to manage access permissions for stored secrets, keys, and certificates, allowing fine-grained control over who can manage and access sensitive information.

244. **Answer:** B

Explanation: Azure Traffic Manager is a DNS-based traffic load balancer that enables you to distribute user traffic across multiple Azure regions to improve the availability, performance, and resilience of your applications.

245. **Answer:** C

Explanation: Entra ID Multi-Factor Authentication (MFA) adds an extra layer of security by requiring users to verify their identity using a second authentication factor, such as a phone call, text message, or mobile app notification, in addition to their password.

246. Answer: C

Explanation: Azure Application Gateway is a web traffic load balancer that provides application-level (Layer 7) load balancing, SSL termination, and web application firewall (WAF) capabilities to optimize and secure your web applications running on Azure.

247. Answer: B

Explanation: Azure Functions is a serverless compute service that allows you to run event-triggered code or scripts without managing infrastructure. It enables you to automate business processes, integrate systems, and respond to events with scalable and cost-effective execution.

248. Answer: B

Explanation: Azure Content Delivery Network (CDN) accelerates the delivery of static and dynamic web content, videos, and applications to users worldwide with reduced latency and improved performance by caching content at strategically placed edge locations.

249. Answer: C

Explanation: Azure Reserved Instances offer significant cost savings (up to 72%) compared to pay-as-you-go pricing for long-term commitments to Azure virtual machines, allowing you to optimize costs for predictable and sustained workloads.

250. Answer: B

Explanation: Azure SQL Database is a fully managed relational database service in Azure that offers built-in high availability, automated backups, and intelligent performance optimization without the need to manage infrastructure. It supports SQL Server workloads and provides scalability and security features tailored for cloud applications.

251. Answer: B

Explanation: Azure DevOps provides tools and services for collaborative software development and delivery, including version control, agile planning, and CI/CD pipelines. It automates build, test, and deployment processes to streamline application lifecycle management and ensure faster delivery of software updates and features.

252. Answer: B

Explanation: Azure Network Security Groups (NSGs) allow you to filter inbound and outbound network traffic to control access to Azure resources based on source and destination IP addresses, ports, and protocols, helping you enforce network security policies and restrict unauthorized access.

253. Answer: B

Explanation: Azure Kubernetes Service (AKS) is a managed Kubernetes orchestration service that simplifies the deployment, management, and scaling of containerized applications using Kubernetes. It offers built-in monitoring, automatic upgrades, and integration with Azure services for seamless container orchestration and management.

254. Answer: B

Explanation: Azure Logic Apps is a serverless integration service that allows you to automate workflows and integrate applications, data, and services across cloud and on-premises environments using a visual designer and pre-built connectors.

255. Answer: B

Explanation: Azure Data Lake Storage Gen2 is optimized for storing large amounts of unstructured data with varying access patterns. It offers high performance, scalability, and cost-efficiency for big data analytics workloads.

256. **Answer:** B

Explanation: Azure Bastion provides secure and seamless RDP and SSH access to Azure virtual machines (VMs) over SSL/TLS without exposing public IP addresses or requiring VPN connections, enhancing security posture and simplifying remote access management.

257. **Answer:** B

Explanation: Azure Resource Groups are containers that hold related Azure resources for management, billing, and access control purposes. They help organize resources, apply policies, and manage them as a single unit.

258. **Answer:** C

Explanation: An Azure App Service Plan defines the pricing tier, scaling, and hosting features (such as VM size, instances, and region) for Azure App Service web apps, mobile apps, and API apps.

259. **Answer:** D

Explanation: Azure Ultra Disk offers the lowest latency and highest performance disk type, suitable for I/O-intensive workloads requiring consistent low latency and high throughput.

260. **Answer:** B

Explanation: Azure Backup retention policy defines how long backup data (recovery points) for Azure VMs, files, and databases is retained before it's automatically deleted.

261. **Answer:** B

Explanation: Azure SQL Managed Instance provides a fully managed instance of SQL Server with near 100% compatibility, enabling easy lift-and-shift migrations of SQL Server applications to Azure.

262. **Answer:** D

Explanation: Azure Traffic Manager supports multiple routing methods, including round-robin, least connections, priority, and geographic proximity, to distribute user traffic across multiple Azure regions or endpoints.

263. **Answer:** D

Explanation: Read-access geo-redundant storage (RA-GRS) replicates data to a secondary region, providing high durability, availability, and read access to data even if the primary region is unavailable.

264. **Answer:** A

Explanation: Azure Functions can be triggered by HTTP requests, events in Azure Blob Storage, timer-based schedules, and various other Azure services and external sources.

265. **Answer:** C

Explanation: AKS is a managed Kubernetes service that offers high availability, scalability, and auto-scaling capabilities. It is well-suited for hosting web applications with fluctuating traffic patterns, as it can automatically adjust the number of instances based on demand.

266. **Answer:** B

Explanation: Azure Policy helps enforce compliance with organizational standards, regulatory requirements, and best practices by applying rules and policies to Azure resources and monitoring their compliance status.

267. **Answer:** C

Explanation: Azure Container Instances (ACI) enables serverless container deployments without managing virtual machines or orchestration infrastructure, suitable for microservices, batch jobs, and CI/CD workflows.

268. **Answer:** C

Explanation: An Azure Policy definition specifies rules and requirements that Azure resources must meet, such as allowed resource types, required tags, and configuration settings, to enforce governance and compliance standards.

269. **Answer:** A

Explanation: Azure VPN Gateway supports site-to-site VPN connections, allowing you to establish secure and reliable connectivity between on-premises networks and Azure virtual networks over the public internet.

270. **Answer:** C

Explanation: Azure Stream Analytics is a fully managed serverless service designed for the real-time processing of streaming data. It enables you to analyze and process data as it arrives, making it suitable for high-volume, low-latency scenarios.

271. **Answer:** C

Explanation: Microsoft Defender for Cloud provides security recommendations based on industry best practices, compliance requirements, and threat intelligence to help remediate vulnerabilities and improve the security posture of Azure resources.

272. Answer: B

Explanation: Azure Site Recovery supports replication and failover scenarios between Azure VMs within the same Azure region or across different Azure regions, providing disaster recovery and business continuity for virtualized workloads.

273. Answer: D

Explanation: Azure Bastion provides secure RDP and SSH connectivity to Azure VMs over SSL/TLS without exposing public IP addresses, ensuring network isolation and reducing exposure to attacks.

274. Answer: B

Explanation: Azure Service Health alerts notify you about planned maintenance events, service incidents, and other events impacting the availability of your Azure resources, helping you stay informed and take necessary actions.

275. Answer: B

Explanation: Applying NSGs to subnet interfaces provides granular control over network traffic for specific subnets within a VNet. This approach is more efficient and secure than applying NSGs to individual VMs or the VNet level.

276. Answer: C

Explanation: Azure DevOps pipelines automate build, test, and deployment processes to enable continuous integration and delivery

(CI/CD) for applications and services, ensuring rapid and reliable software delivery.

277. Answer: A

Explanation: Azure Policy allows you to enforce governance and compliance requirements across your Azure subscriptions by defining rules and policies, such as requiring specific tags on resources.

278. Answer: B

Explanation: Azure Kubernetes Service (AKS) provides managed Kubernetes orchestration to deploy, manage, and scale containerized applications. It integrates with Entra ID for identity and access management and supports automated scaling based on metrics like CPU utilization.

279. Answer: B

Explanation: Azure Virtual WAN provides optimized and automated branch-to-branch connectivity and connectivity to Azure services using a hub-and-spoke topology. It is suitable for securely connecting multiple branch offices worldwide.

280. Answer: B

Explanation: Azure Data Factory is a fully managed data integration service that allows you to create, schedule, and orchestrate data pipelines for data movement and transformation across various Azure and on-premises data sources.

281. Answer: B

Explanation: Azure Site Recovery (ASR) provides disaster recovery as a service (DRaaS) by orchestrating replication, failover, and failback of on-premises virtual machines (VMs) and Azure VMs to ensure business continuity during disruptions.

282. **Answer:** B

Explanation: Azure Firewall supports application rules that allow or deny outbound traffic based on FQDN tags or IP addresses. To allow outbound traffic to specific IP addresses and deny all others, you would create application rules specifying the allowed IPs.

283. **Answer:** C

Explanation: Azure Storage Service Encryption (SSE) automatically encrypts data at rest in Azure Blob Storage using Microsoft-managed keys. To use customer-managed keys from Azure Key Vault, you would enable customer-managed keys for SSE.

284. **Answer:** D

Explanation: The Build task in Azure DevOps allows you to build and package applications, including .NET Core applications, and publish artifacts to be deployed in subsequent stages of the CI/CD pipeline.

285. **Answer:** C

Explanation: Azure SQL Database supports read-scale-out using read replicas (also known as read replicas), which allow you to offload read-heavy workloads to secondary replicas while maintaining the primary database for write operations, optimizing performance and cost.

286. **Answer:** A

Explanation: Azure NSGs allow you to define inbound and outbound security rules to control network traffic to and from Azure resources based on source and destination IP addresses, ports, and protocols.

287. **Answer:** B

Explanation: Azure Virtual Network peering enables direct VM-to-VM communication across Azure VNets, including those connected to on-premises networks via Azure ExpressRoute, without needing to route traffic through the public internet.

288. **Answer:** D

Explanation: Azure Log Analytics is a powerful platform for collecting, analyzing, and visualizing log data from various Azure resources. It provides advanced analytics capabilities and integration with other Azure services.

289. **Answer:** D

Explanation: Azure Key Vault RBAC (Role-Based Access Control) allows you to grant permissions to Azure services and users to access secrets and keys stored in Key Vault without exposing sensitive information, ensuring secure access management.

290. **Answer:** B

Explanation: An Internal Load Balancer in Azure provides load balancing within a virtual network (VNet) and ensures high availability by distributing traffic to multiple VM instances based on configured rules and health probes.

291. **Answer:** C

Explanation: Azure Policy Initiative allows you to group and enforce a set of Azure policies as a single unit across multiple Azure subscriptions and management groups, simplifying governance and compliance management.

292. **Answer:** C

Explanation: Configuring a service principal with a certificate in Kubernetes allows secure authentication to Azure Container Registry (ACR) for pulling container images without exposing credentials, ensuring secure access management.

293. **Answer:** A

Explanation: Active geo-replication in Azure SQL Database asynchronously replicates committed transactions from the primary database to one or more secondary databases in different Azure regions for disaster recovery and failover capabilities.

294. **Answer:** B

Explanation: Geographic routing in Azure Traffic Manager directs user traffic based on the geographic location of the DNS resolver making the query, routing users to the nearest datacenter or endpoint location for improved performance and user experience.

295. **Answer:** D

Explanation: Azure Functions can leverage the Azure App Service Authentication/Authorization feature to authenticate and authorize users using Entra ID identities, allowing secure access to HTTP-triggered function endpoints.

296. **Answer:** B

Explanation: The Cool access tier in Azure Storage is suitable for data that is infrequently accessed (at least 30 days between access), offering lower storage costs compared to the Hot access tier while maintaining flexible latency requirements.

297. **Answer:** B

Explanation: Azure Resource Manager (ARM) is the deployment and management service for Azure. It provides a management layer that enables you to create, update, and delete resources in your Azure account. ARM also manages the dependencies between resources, such as ensuring that a web app is associated with an Azure App Service plan. While ARM helps with resource organization and deployment, it does not handle Azure subscriptions and billing directly, nor does it provide networking services.

298. **Answer:** B

Explanation: Azure Blob storage is used to store large amounts of unstructured object data, such as text or binary data. It provides three access tiers: Hot, Cool, and Archive, allowing you to optimize costs based on how frequently data is accessed.

299. **Answer:** C

Explanation: Azure App Services is a fully managed platform for building, deploying, and scaling web applications and APIs. It supports multiple programming languages and frameworks and provides integration with Azure DevOps for continuous deployment.

300. **Answer:** C

Explanation: Azure Application Gateway is a scalable and highly available Application Delivery Controller (ADC) that provides layer 7 load balancing, SSL termination, and URL-based routing for HTTP/HTTPS traffic.

301. **Answer:** D

Explanation: The core concepts of Azure RBAC (Role-Based Access Control) include Security Principal, Role Definition, Scope, and Role Assignment. A Security Principal represents the user, group, service principal, or managed identity requesting access to Azure resources. A Role Definition is a collection of permissions that can be performed, and Scope specifies the set of resources that the access applies to. A Role Assignment links a Role Definition to a Security Principal at a specified Scope. Load Balancer, however, is not a core concept of Azure RBAC.

302. Answer: C

Explanation: The Owner role grants full access to manage all resources, including the ability to assign roles in Azure RBAC. The Contributor role has full access to manage resources but cannot assign roles. The Reader role only allows viewing resources without making any changes. The User Access Administrator role is specific to managing user access.

303. Answer: B

Explanation: In a custom role definition in Azure RBAC, the NotActions permission set specifies what actions are not allowed. Actions permissions identify what actions are allowed, DataActions permissions indicate how data can be changed or used, and AssignableScopes permissions list the scopes where a role definition can be assigned.

304. Answer: C

Explanation: Limiting the access scope to the minimum required for job duties helps in maintaining security. Assigning all users as Owners or allowing unrestricted data modifications can lead to security risks. While using built-in roles can be beneficial, it is often necessary to create custom roles to meet specific business needs.

305. Answer: B

Explanation: The primary purpose of a role assignment is to control access. It involves scoping a role definition to limit permissions for a requestor, such as a user, group, service principal, or managed identity.

306. Answer: B

Explanation: The Contributor role can create and manage all types of Azure resources but cannot grant access to others. This role is designed for users who need to manage resources without having the ability to assign roles to other users.

307. Answer: C

Explanation: Guest users have the most restricted level of access in Microsoft Entra ID. They are typically invited to collaborate with the organization and have limited permissions compared to member and administrator accounts.

308. Answer: B

Explanation: The command `New-MgUser` is used in Azure PowerShell to create a new user. This cmdlet is part of the Microsoft Graph PowerShell module, which is used for managing Microsoft Entra resources.

309. Answer: A

Explanation: By using Microsoft Entra B2B, organizations do not need to manage and authenticate the identities of external partners. This simplifies collaboration, as partners can use their existing identities managed by their organization.

310. Answer: D

Explanation: Rule-based assignment uses rules to determine group membership based on user or device properties. If the rules are met, the user or device is added to the group; if not, they are removed.

311. Answer: B

Explanation: Microsoft Entra Connect allows employees to manage their Azure subscriptions using their existing work identities by extending on-premises Active Directory to the cloud. This integration ensures a seamless identity and access management experience, enabling users to access cloud resources with their familiar on-premises credentials enhancing security and productivity.

312. Answer: B

Explanation: Azure RBAC does not inherently provide a way for external users to manage Azure resources without an invitation or proper role assignment. External users need to be invited and assigned roles appropriately.

313. Answer: B

Explanation: In Azure RBAC, a security principal refers to the entity to which you want to grant access. This can be a user, a group, or an application. Security principals are essential in defining who can access specific resources and what actions they can perform within the Azure environment.

314. Answer: C

Explanation: The Owner role in Azure RBAC has full access to all resources, including the right to delegate access to others. It is one of the fundamental built-in roles provided by Azure, allowing comprehensive control over resources within a subscription.

315. Answer: C

Explanation: Scope in Azure RBAC determines the level where the access applies, such as management group, subscription, resource group, or resource. Child scopes inherit permissions granted at a parent scope.

316. Answer: C

Explanation: 'NotActions' permissions in Azure RBAC are used to define a set of operations that are not allowed, effectively subtracting them from the Actions operations to compute the effective permissions of a role.

317. Answer: B

Explanation: Self-Service Password Reset (SSPR) allows users to reset their passwords without needing to contact help-desk support, thereby reducing the workload on support staff and decreasing help-desk costs.

318. Answer: B

Explanation: Self-Service Password Reset (SSPR) supports several authentication methods, including mobile app notifications, security questions, and email, but it does not support fingerprint scans.

319. Answer: B

Explanation: In Azure Self-Service Password Reset (SSPR), users are required to register at least two authentication methods to ensure they have multiple ways to verify their identity if they forget their password. This enhances security by providing alternative verification methods.

320. Answer: D

Explanation: Self-service password reset is available to users who are not signed in and have forgotten their password or whose password has expired in Microsoft Entra ID Premium P1, Premium P2, and Microsoft 365 Apps for business.

321. Answer: B

Explanation: Azure Blob Storage is designed to handle unstructured data, which is the least organized and may not have a clear relationship. This makes it ideal for storing large amounts of text or binary data, such as images, videos, and backup files.

322. **Answer:** C

Explanation: Azure File Storage provides fully managed file shares in the cloud, suitable for usage with IaaS virtual machines and various applications. It offers shared access to files, supports SMB and NFS protocols, and integrates seamlessly with both cloud and on-premises environments.

323. **Answer:** C

Explanation: Premium storage accounts are backed by solid-state drives (SSD) and offer consistent low-latency performance, making them ideal for I/O-intensive applications like databases.

324. **Answer:** D

Explanation: Structured data is organized in a relational format, where information is stored in tables with rows and columns. This data type adheres to a predefined schema that defines the structure and relationships between different data elements.

325. **Answer:** B

Explanation: Azure Blob Storage is a highly scalable, REST-based cloud object store used for storing unstructured data. It is ideal for storing massive amounts of unstructured data, such as text or binary data, and is optimized for serving images or documents directly to a browser. Blob Storage supports hot, cool, and archive tiers, allowing users to manage their costs and access requirements efficiently.

326. **Answer:** B

Explanation: Azure Table Storage is an autoscaling NoSQL store used for storing structured data in a non-relational format. It allows developers to store large amounts of structured data, providing a key/attribute store with a schema-less design. This makes it particularly suitable for applications that require flexible data structures, such as user profiles, device information, or any other metadata that needs to be queried quickly and at scale.

327. **Answer:** B

Explanation: Azure Data Lake Storage is used for storing unstructured data and is based on the Hadoop Distributed File System (HDFS). It is designed to handle large volumes of data, making it perfect for big data analytics. This service allows organizations to capture data of any size, type, and ingestion speed in a single place for operational and exploratory analytics.

328. **Answer:** C

Explanation: Azure Storage is known for its scalability, durability, high availability, and secure access with encryption. It is designed to scale up or down according to the needs of the application. Therefore, "Limited scalability" is not a feature of Azure Storage.

329. **Answer:** C

Explanation: Each data disk used by Azure virtual machines has a maximum capacity of 32,767 GB. This allows users to attach large volumes to their VMs, accommodating applications that require significant storage, such as databases or big data processing.

330. **Answer:** B

Explanation: Azure Storage ensures that data is accessible globally over HTTP or HTTPS, making it easily reachable from anywhere in the world. This global accessibility is achieved through Azure's robust networking infrastructure, which includes multiple data centers around the world, enabling low-latency access and high availability for users, regardless of their geographical location.

331. **Answer:** D

Explanation: Azure Blob Storage is optimized for storing massive amounts of unstructured or nonrelational data, such as text or binary data. This makes it ideal for scenarios like serving documents or media files directly to users via web browsers.

332. **Answer:** C

Explanation: Azure Files can be accessed using the Server Message Block (SMB) protocol, as well as the Network File System (NFS) protocol. This allows seamless integration with on-premises environments and supports lift-and-shift scenarios for existing applications.

333. **Answer:** C

Explanation: Queue messages in Azure Queue Storage can be up to 64 KB in size. This is suitable for tasks that require passing relatively small messages between components in a distributed application for asynchronous processing.

334. **Answer:** D

Explanation: Azure Table Storage is ideal for storing non-relational structured data, providing a key/attribute store with a schemaless design. It is particularly well-suited for scenarios where the application needs to store large amounts of structured but non-relational data.

335. **Answer:** B

Explanation: Azure Files enables you to set up highly available network file shares that multiple virtual machines can access. This makes it a good fit for applications that require shared access to files and directories.

336. **Answer:** D

Explanation: Objects in Blob Storage can be accessed via URLs, the Azure Storage REST API, Azure PowerShell, the Azure CLI, or an Azure Storage client library. This flexibility allows developers to choose the most suitable access method for their applications.

337. **Answer:** C

Explanation: Azure Queue Storage is commonly used to store lists of messages to be processed asynchronously, creating a backlog of work. This helps in decoupling application components and enables reliable message delivery for background processing tasks.

238. **Answer:** D

Explanation: Access to Table storage data is fast and cost-effective for many types of applications and is typically lower in cost than traditional SQL databases for similar volumes of data. It is optimized for large-scale, high-availability, and low-cost access to non-relational structured data.

339. **Answer:** B

Explanation: Regularly rotating and regenerating access keys is a best practice to enhance security by minimizing the risk of unauthorized access if a key is compromised.

340. **Answer:** A

Explanation: By mounting the file share to the same drive letter that the on-premises application uses, the application can work with minimal changes during migration. This simplifies the process of migrating applications to Azure by maintaining the existing file path references.

341. Answer: B

Explanation: Azure Virtual Machine Scale Sets are designed to deploy and manage a set of identical virtual machines with the ability to automatically scale based on application demand. This means that the number of virtual machines can increase as demand goes up and decrease as demand goes down, ensuring efficient resource use.

342. Answer: C

Explanation: Azure Virtual Machine Scale Sets support the use of Azure Load Balancer for basic layer-4 traffic distribution and Azure Application Gateway for more advanced layer-7 traffic distribution and SSL termination, providing flexibility in handling different types of traffic for applications.

343. Answer: B

Explanation: When using custom virtual machine images, Azure Virtual Machine Scale Sets support up to 600 virtual machine instances. This is lower than the 1,000 instance limit when using base operating system images, reflecting the additional complexity and resources involved in managing custom images.

344. Answer: B

Explanation: In flexible orchestration mode, you can manually create and add virtual machines with any configuration to the scale set. In uniform orchestration mode, you define a virtual machine model, and Azure generates identical instances based on that model.

345. Answer: B

Explanation: Azure Spot offers unused Azure capacity at a discounted rate versus pay-as-you-go prices. However, workloads should be tolerant to infrastructure loss as Azure may recall the capacity.

346. **Answer:** C

Explanation: Under the Advanced tab, you can select "Enable scaling beyond 100 instances." If you select Yes, your implementation can span multiple placement groups with a capacity of up to 1,000, whereas selecting No limits your implementation to one placement group with a maximum capacity of 100.

347. **Answer:** B

Explanation: Autoscaling allows the number of virtual machines in your implementation to automatically increase or decrease based on the current workload demands. This ensures optimal performance and cost efficiency by scaling out during high demand and scaling in during low demand.

348. **Answer:** C

Explanation: The "Scale-out CPU threshold" setting specifies the CPU usage percentage that triggers the scale-out autoscale rule, causing additional virtual machines to be added to handle increased load.

349. **Answer:** C

Explanation: The 'duration in minutes' setting determines how far back the autoscale engine looks at metrics to make scaling decisions. This delay helps stabilize metrics and avoids reacting to brief, transient spikes in demand.

350. **Answer:** B

Explanation: Azure Backup offers a straightforward, secure, and cost-efficient way to back up data and ensure its recovery from the Microsoft

VERSAtile Reads

Azure cloud. Its simplicity comes from the easy setup and management interfaces, security is maintained through encryption and compliance with industry standards, and cost-effectiveness is achieved through flexible pricing models that scale with your needs.

351. **Answer:** D

Explanation: Azure Backup is designed to protect Azure resources such as Virtual Machines, SQL and SAP databases, Azure file shares, and blobs. It does not extend its backup capabilities to Google Cloud Storage or other non-Azure cloud services, focusing instead on Microsoft's ecosystem.

352. **Answer:** C

Explanation: Azure Backup's centralized management interface simplifies the process of creating and managing backup policies. This feature allows users to set up automated backups, define retention policies, and configure data protection strategies for a variety of enterprise workloads, streamlining backup operations and ensuring consistency across different data sources.

353. **Answer:** B

Explanation: Azure Backup offers a zero-infrastructure backup solution, which means that you don't need to deploy or maintain additional backup infrastructure. It leverages Azure's cloud infrastructure to manage and store backups, providing a hassle-free backup experience for all Azure-managed data assets without requiring on-premises hardware or software.

354. **Answer:** D

Explanation: Azure Backup can provide backup services for on-premises files, folders, and system state, Azure Virtual Machines (VMs), Azure Managed Disks, Azure Files Shares, SQL Server in Azure VMs, SAP HANA databases in Azure VMs, Azure Database for PostgreSQL servers, Azure

Blobs, Azure Database for PostgreSQL-Flexible servers, Azure Database for MySQL-Flexible servers, and Azure Kubernetes clusters.

355. Answer: B

Explanation: The Azure Import/Export tool is used to prepare your data for an import or export job. This tool helps you copy data to the drives, encrypt it, and generate the required journal files.

356. Answer: C

Explanation: The Backup Center in Azure Backup enables you to natively manage your entire backup estate from a central console. It helps you discover, govern, monitor, operate, and optimize backup management, driving operational efficiency.

357. Answer: B

Explanation: An RPO (Recovery Point Objective) of one hour means backups are performed every hour, ensuring that no more than one hour of data is lost in the event of a data loss incident. An RTO (Recovery Time Objective) of three hours means the system must be restored within three hours to minimize the impact on operations.

358. Answer: C

Explanation: Azure Backup is designed to back up data, machine state, and workloads from both on-premises machines and Azure VM instances to the Azure cloud. This ensures that data is protected and can be restored in case of data loss or corruption.

359. Answer: B

Explanation: Azure Backup supports a variety of backup types, including full backups, incremental backups, and specific SQL Server backup types (full, differential, and transaction log backups). This allows for flexible and efficient data protection strategies.

360. **Answer:** C

Explanation: In Azure Backup, a vault is an online storage entity that holds backup copies, recovery points, and backup policies. It serves as the main interface for users to interact with the backup service and manage their backup data.

361. **Answer:** B

Explanation: Selective Disk Backup is a feature in Azure Backup that allows you to back up only a subset of the data disks attached to your VM. This helps in managing critical data efficiently and can reduce costs by not backing up unnecessary disks.

362. **Answer:** B

Explanation: The Snapshot tier allows for faster restores because the snapshot is stored locally in the customer's subscription, eliminating the wait time for snapshots to be copied from the vault before the restore operation can begin.

363. **Answer:** C

Explanation: The Archive tier in Azure Storage is specifically designed for storing infrequently accessed or "cold" data, such as older backup files. It offers a lower storage cost compared to the Hot and Cool tiers, making it ideal for long-term data retention where the data is rarely accessed but needs to be kept for compliance or archival purposes. The Archive tier provides significant cost savings but has higher access latency and retrieval costs.

364. **Answer:** B

Explanation: Azure Backup's soft-delete feature allows for the retention of deleted backups for 14 additional days free of charge. This ensures that if a backup is accidentally or maliciously deleted, it can still be recovered within this period, providing an extra layer of protection and helping to safeguard against unintended data loss.

365. **Answer:** A

Explanation: The Recovery Services vault, also known as the Backup vault, is a crucial component in Azure Backup. It provides a centralized interface for managing backup and recovery operations, including defining backup policies, configuring backup schedules, and storing backup data. This vault serves as the primary container for all backup data and operations, enabling efficient and organized management of backup resources.

366. **Answer:** B

Explanation: Zone-Redundant Storage (ZRS) ensures that data is replicated synchronously across different availability zones within a single region, providing protection against zone failures.

367. **Answer:** C

Explanation: Activity log alerts in Azure Monitor are used to notify you of specific changes or events that occur within Azure resources. These alerts can be triggered by events such as the creation, modification, or deletion of resources or other significant state changes. They help you stay informed about critical operational changes and maintain oversight of your Azure environment.

368. **Answer:** C

Explanation: Azure Monitor categorizes alerts into five severity levels to prioritize response and action. The levels are 0 for Critical (urgent issues that need immediate attention), 1 for Error (issues causing significant problems but not critical), 2 for Warning (potential issues that could develop into more serious problems), 3 for Informational (status updates or general information), and 4 for Verbose (detailed diagnostic information useful for in-depth troubleshooting).

369. **Answer:** C

Explanation: In Azure Monitor, an action group is a collection of notification and automation settings that define who should be alerted and how. Each action group typically includes a unique set of recipients, such as email addresses, SMS numbers, or webhook URLs, to ensure that alerts are directed to the appropriate individuals or systems. This customization allows for effective and targeted responses to alert conditions.

370. **Answer:** B

Explanation: Static threshold metric alerts are configured based on fixed thresholds that you define. For example, you might set an alert to trigger if CPU usage exceeds 85% for a specified period. These alerts are straightforward and do not adapt to changing conditions; they operate based on predefined static values, providing clear and predictable monitoring for specific conditions.

371. **Answer:** B

Explanation: Dynamic threshold metric alerts leverage machine learning to adapt to changing conditions by defining a look-back period and the number of violations needed to trigger an alert. The look-back period is the timeframe over which historical data is analyzed. At the same time, the number of violations specifies how many deviations from the expected behavior are required before an alert is triggered. This approach allows for more flexible and intelligent alerting based on evolving patterns.

372. **Answer:** B

Explanation: Dimensions in Azure Monitor allow you to apply a single metric alert rule across multiple instances of a resource, such as virtual machines or databases. By defining dimensions, you can aggregate and monitor data from various instances collectively, making it easier to manage and respond to performance or health issues that affect multiple resources simultaneously.

373. **Answer:** B

Explanation: Static threshold metric alerts in Azure Monitor work by continuously assessing data from the last defined period (e.g., the last 10 minutes) and checking the alert rule at regular intervals (e.g., every two minutes). If the monitored metric exceeds the predefined threshold during these checks, an alert is triggered. This regular interval evaluation ensures timely detection of threshold breaches and prompt notification.

374. **Answer:** B

Explanation: Log alerts in Azure Monitor are considered stateless because each alert is generated independently based on the current data that matches the rule criteria. This means that each time the rule's conditions are met, a new alert is created without considering previous alerts or alert history. This approach is useful for monitoring real-time data and capturing every instance of an event that matches the criteria.

375. **Answer:** D

Explanation: RA-GRS provides the highest level of durability and availability by replicating data across multiple regions. It also allows for read access to the data in the secondary region, even if the primary region becomes unavailable.

376. **Answer:** C

Explanation: In Azure Monitor, a log search rule is configured using a log query, which defines the specific search criteria for the logs. Along with the query, you set parameters such as the time range for the query, how often the query should run, and the threshold that triggers an alert. This setup allows for detailed and customizable monitoring of log data.

377. **Answer:** C

Explanation: Specific operations alerts in Azure Monitor are designed to notify you about particular changes or actions occurring within your Azure resources. For example, an alert might be triggered if a new role is assigned to a user, indicating a change in permissions or configurations. These alerts are useful for tracking and auditing specific activities in your environment.

378. **Answer:** C

Explanation: When setting up a service health alert in Azure Monitor, the alert can be configured to cover a whole Azure region rather than targeting individual resources. This allows you to be notified about service health issues that impact an entire region, providing a broader view of potential outages or disruptions affecting your resources.

379. **Answer:** C

Explanation: In activity log alerts, the "Level" attribute refers to the severity of the logged event. This attribute categorizes events into different levels, such as verbose, informational, warning, error, and critical. It helps prioritize alerts based on the severity of the event, allowing for more effective monitoring and response.

380. **Answer:** C

Explanation: Azure Data Box is a service designed to transfer large amounts of data to and from Azure using physical disks. This service is ideal for scenarios where transferring data over the network would be too slow or costly.

381. **Answer:** D

Explanation: Azure Monitor action groups can perform actions such as sending emails, restarting VMs, and creating ITSM tickets, but they cannot modify subscription billing preferences.

382. **Answer:** B

Explanation: The Azure Import/Export service is used to securely move large amounts of data to and from Azure using physical hard drives, which are shipped to a Microsoft data center for uploading or downloading.

383. **Answer:** B

Explanation: Azure Monitor Metrics collects numerical values at predetermined intervals to describe aspects like VM performance, resource utilization, error counts, and user responses. This data helps in monitoring and managing VM performance.

384. **Answer:** C

Explanation: Activity logs can be sent to Azure Monitor Logs for more complex querying and alerting. This allows for in-depth analysis and longer retention, up to two years.

385. **Answer:** C

Explanation: Azure automatically collects basic metrics such as CPU usage percentage, network operations, and disk operations per second for VM hosts. Application error counts are not included in these basic metrics.

386. **Answer:** C

Explanation: Metrics Explorer enables users to plot multiple metrics on a graph, investigate changes, and visually correlate metrics trends for VMs. It offers flexibility in time ranges, granularity, and other settings.

387. **Answer:** B

Explanation: Boot diagnostics provide host logs and screenshots from the VM's hypervisor to help troubleshoot boot issues. It can display serial console log output for Linux machines and is enabled by default or configured afterward.

388. **Answer:** A

Explanation: To collect metrics and logs from the guest operating system (OS) and client applications running on a virtual machine (VM), you must install the Azure Monitor Agent (AMA). The AMA is designed to gather data from VMs and other resources and send it to Azure Monitor. You also need to set up a Data Collection Rule (DCR) to specify which data to collect and how to process it.

389. **Answer:** B

Explanation: Azure Monitor Logs is a service that can store and query both metrics and event logs, offering comprehensive insights into your resources. In contrast, Azure Monitor Metrics is specialized for storing time-series data related to performance metrics only. Azure Monitor Logs uses a more versatile storage solution, accommodating a broader range of data types.

390. **Answer:** B

Explanation: VM Insights simplifies the onboarding process for the Azure Monitor Agent by streamlining the setup and configuration needed to monitor a VM's guest OS and workloads. This feature helps users quickly deploy the monitoring solution with minimal manual setup, ensuring that the VM is effectively monitored.

391. **Answer:** B

Explanation: VM Insights can collect data on the processes running on a VM. This includes information about the processes themselves and their dependencies on other services. This data helps in understanding the performance and operational state of applications running within the VM, providing valuable insights for troubleshooting and optimization.

392. **Answer:** C

Explanation: Kusto Query Language (KQL) is used to write log queries for analyzing data stored in a Log Analytics workspace. KQL allows users to perform complex queries and data manipulations, making it a powerful tool for gaining insights from logs and metrics collected by Azure Monitor.

393. **Answer:** C

Explanation: The first step in managing or configuring VMs in Azure is to sign in to the Azure portal. From there, you can use the search functionality to locate the "Virtual Machines" section, where you can view and manage your VM instances.

394. **Answer:** B

Explanation: When creating a new VM, you need to select an appropriate image. For the scenario described, Ubuntu Server 20.04 LTS-x64 Gen2 is specified, which is a stable and widely used version of the Ubuntu operating system optimized for Azure.

395. **Answer:** B

Explanation: For diagnostics, enabling Boot diagnostics with a managed storage account is recommended. This configuration ensures that boot logs and other diagnostic data are stored securely and are easily accessible for troubleshooting purposes.

396. **Answer:** D

Explanation: In the Azure portal, the option to "Enable recommended alert rules" can be found under the Monitoring tab. This tab provides access to various monitoring settings and configurations, including alert rules that help in tracking and responding to potential issues with the VM.

397. **Answer:** B

Explanation: To view the activity log for a VM, you should navigate to the VM's left-hand menu in the Azure portal and select "Activity log." This section provides a detailed record of all actions and changes made to the VM, helping in tracking operations and diagnosing

398. **Answer:** B

Explanation: The Azure Monitor Agent (AMA) is responsible for collecting data from inside the virtual machine (VM), including details about the software and processes running on it. This agent provides comprehensive monitoring capabilities, allowing for deep insights into the performance and health of applications and services within the VM.

399. **Answer:** B

Explanation: VM Insights simplifies the process of monitoring VMs by creating a Data Collection Rule (DCR) that automatically gathers and sends a predefined set of client performance data to a Log Analytics workspace. This setup helps in efficiently tracking performance metrics and operational data without manual configuration of each data collection aspect.

400. **Answer:** C

Explanation: On the Monitoring configuration page within the Azure portal, it is recommended to install the Azure Monitor Agent. This recommendation ensures that the VM is set up with the appropriate tools for comprehensive monitoring and data collection, enabling effective tracking and analysis of performance and health metrics.

About Our Products

Other products from VERSAtile Reads are:

 Elevate Your Leadership: The 10 Must-Have Skills

 Elevate Your Leadership: 8 Effective Communication Skills

 Elevate Your Leadership: 10 Leadership Styles for Every Situation

 300+ PMP Practice Questions Aligned with PMBOK 7, Agile Methods, and Key Process Groups – 2024

 Exam-Cram Essentials Last-Minute Guide to Ace the PMP Exam - Your Express Guide featuring PMBOK® Guide

 Career Mastery Blueprint - Strategies for Success in Work and Business

 Memory Magic: Unraveling the Secret of Mind Mastery

 The Success Equation Psychological Foundations For Accomplishment

 Fairy Dust Chronicles – The Short and Sweet of Wonder

 B2B Breakthrough – Proven Strategies from Real-World Case Studies

CISSP Fast Track Master: CISSP Essentials for Exam Success

 CISA Fast Track Master: CISA Essentials for Exam Success

 CISM Fast Track Master: CISM Essentials for Exam Success

 CCSP Fast Track Master: CCSP Essentials for Exam Success

 CLF-C02: AWS Certified Cloud Practitioner: Fast Track to Exam Success

 ITIL 4 Foundation Essentials: Fast Track to Exam Success

 CCNP Security Essentials: Fast Track to Exam Success

 Certified SCRUM Master Exam Cram Essentials

 Six Sigma Green Belt Exam Cram: Essentials for Exam Success

 Microsoft 365 Fundamentals: Fast Track to Exam Success

 AZ-900 Essentials: Fast Track to Exam Success